Über	Regarding
Über	Regarding
Über	Regarding
Über	Regarding
Über	

Raum
und
und
und
und
und
und

　　　　　　　　　　　　　　　　　　Space
　　　　　　　　　　　　　　　　　　and

　　　　　　　　　　　　　　　　　　Spaces
　　　　　　　　　　　　　　　　　　Spaces
　　　　　　　　　　　　　　　　　　Spaces
Räume　　　　　　　　　　　　　　　Spaces
Räume　　　　　　　　　　　　　　　Spaces
Räume　　　　　　　　　　　　　　　Spaces

↑
N

1:500

Über Über Über Über

Regarding Regarding Regarding Regarding Regarding

Kammergrundrisse
und Luca Selva Architekten

Chambered Floor Plans
and Luca Selva Architects

Tilo Richter
Christoph Wieser

Hg./Eds.

Raum und und und und

Space and

Räume Räume Räume Räume Räume

Spaces Spaces Spaces

PARK BOOKS

Über Raum und Räume
Luca Selva

15

Regarding Space and Spaces
Luca Selva

15

Vielfalt in der Einheit
Christoph Wieser

29

Variety in Unity
Christoph Wieser

29

«Wohnen ist immer
eine Summe von Erlebnissen»
Patrick Gmür und Luca Selva

67

"Dwelling Is Always
a Sum of Experiences"
Patrick Gmür and Luca Selva

67

Der Grundriss dieses Museums wirkt offen und fliessend. Durch die Reihung der Schalendächer wird der Raum aber spürbar gegliedert und rhythmisiert. Kimbell Art Museum, Fort Worth, Texas, Louis I. Kahn, 1972.

The floor plan of this museum appears open and flowing. However, the sequence of the shell roofs gives the room a noticeable structure and rhythm. Kimbell Art Museum (1972), Fort Worth, Texas by Louis I. Kahn.

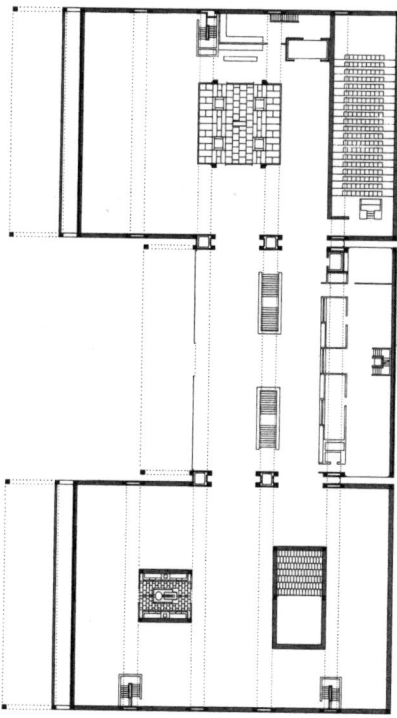

1

Die Siedlung in Çatal Höyük (Türkei, um 7000 v. Chr.) gehört zu den frühesten Beispielen einer rechteckigen Bebauungsstruktur. Gassen und Strassen fehlen, weil die Einraumhäuser über das Dach betreten wurden.

Settlement at Çatalhöyük (Turkey, approx. 7000 BC), one of the earliest examples of a rectangular formal building structure. There were no alleys or streets because the single room houses were entered through the roof.

2

Beim sogenannten Mittelsaalhaus werden die lateralen Kammern über den zentralen Raum erschlossen. Zur Belüftung und Belichtung war er höher als die umliegenden Räume ausgebildet. Mittelsaalhaus mit westlich vorgelagertem Hof in Assur (Irak, um 2200 v. Chr.).

Middle room house with courtyard to the west in Ashur (Iraq, approx. 2200 BC). The lateral chambers are accessed via the central space. To provide for ventilation and daylight exposure, this area was designed to be higher than the surrounding spaces.

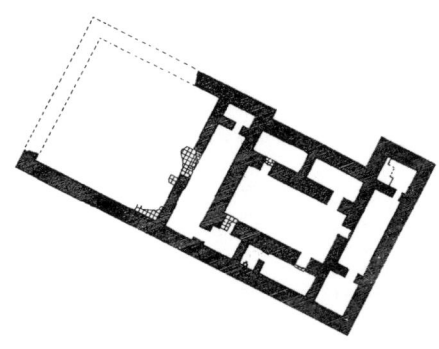

3

Der aus drei Schichten aufgebaute typische Kammergrundriss im urbanen Kontext stellt in jeder Etage nahezu gleichwertige Räume zur Verfügung. Das neusachliche Gebäude ist einer der beiden Köpfe einer kurzen Zeile von drei Mehrfamilienhäusern. Wohnhaus im Bachletten-Quartier, nahe der Pauluskirche, Basel, Georg Stamm, 1930–1932; Umbau: 2014/15.

In an urban context the typical chamber floor plan, organized in three layers, provides nearly equally sized rooms in each story. This New Objectivity building is one of the two head-ends of a short row of three multi-family houses. Residential building in Bachletten Quarter near Pauluskirche, Basel, Georg Stamm, 1930–1932; re-modeling: 2014–2015.

↓ →

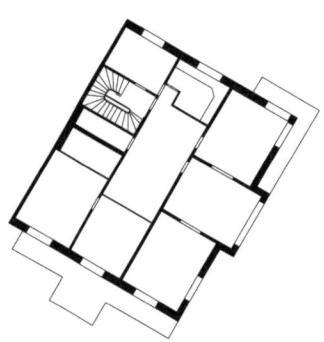

Zwei dreigeschossige Gebäude mit 40 Wohnungen veranschaulichen die Urtypen gekammerter Grundrisse von Luca Selva Architekten. Der «Fussabdruck» von 12 × 25 Metern gab den Impuls für dreispännig angelegte, behutsam ausgewogene Raumschichten, die einmal längs und einmal quer eingestellt sind. Wohnüberbauung Sandfelsen, Erlenbach, Projektwettbewerb im selektiven Verfahren, Gemeinde Erlenbach bei Zürich: 2009.

Two three-story buildings with forty apartments, illustrating the archetypes of chambered floor plans by Luca Selva Architekten. The 12 × 25 meter "footprint" was the basis for a layout with three units per floor and carefully balanced spatial strata, alternately oriented lengthwise and crosswise. Sandfelsen housing development, Erlenbach, invited competition project entry, Municipality of Erlenbach near Zurich: 2009.

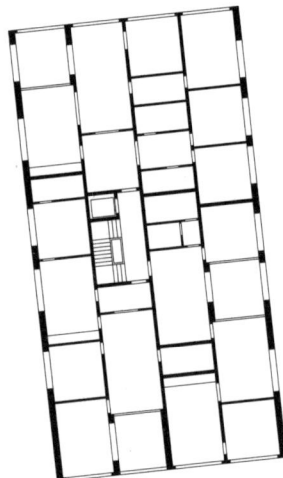

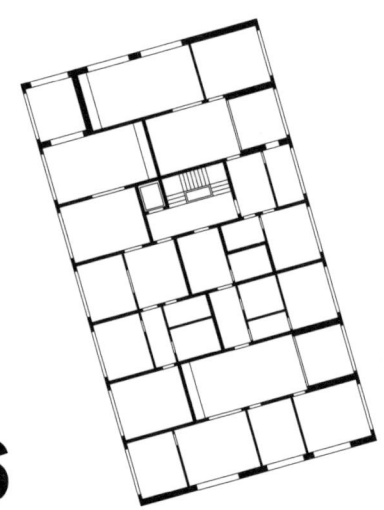

6

Neben den Mittelsaalhäusern brachte die Uruk-Kultur im heutigen Syrien auch die ersten Hofhäuser hervor. Der Hof diente als Verteilraum für die Zimmer und Wirtschaftsräume. Neubabylonisches Haus in Uruk, um 600 v. Chr.

New Babylonian house in Uruk (Syria, approx. 600 BC). In addition to the middle room houses, the Uruk culture also created the first courtyard houses. The courtyard served as a distribution area for the rooms and utility spaces.

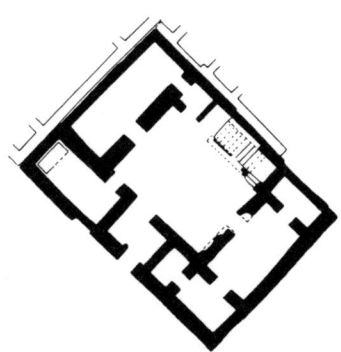

Im Kontext eines gewachsenen Ortskerns mit historischen Baumgärten sollen neue Wohnungen entstehen. Die Studie nimmt mit einem stadträumlich anspruchsvoll komponierten Baukörper die Körnung der Umgebung auf. Das Innere ist geprägt von einem dichten System verschiedenartiger Kammergrundrisse, die sich gekonnt in die Tiefe entwickeln. Zentrumsüberbauung Areal Hübeli, Aesch, Studienauftrag auf Einladung, Bürgergemeinde Aesch BL: 2010.

Planned creation of new apartments within the organic structure of a town center with old orchards. In terms of the urban fabric, the study proposes an ambitious architectural volume adopting the grain of the surroundings. The interior is characterized by a dense system of different chambered floor plans, which are skillfully worked out across the depth of the plot. Town center development, Hübeli Works Site, Aesch, invited study commission, Civic Community Aesch, Canton Basel-Landschaft, 2010.

Auf einem umgenutzten Industrieareal soll ein kompakter Baukörper entstehen, dessen starke formale Repetitionen als Reminiszenz an die Vergangenheit lesbar sind. Zugleich zitieren die Gebäudevolumen die benachbarten Arbeiterwohnhäuser und bilden einen Kontrast zum neu angelegten Park und zum nahen Bodensee. Wohnen am Park, Saurer-Areal «WerkZwei», Arbon, Projektwettbewerb auf Einladung, HRS Real Estate AG: 2013.

To be built on a reused industrial site, the strong formal repetitions of the compact form can be read as reminiscent of the past. At the same time, the architectural volumes cite the neighboring workers housing and establish a contrast to the newly created park and nearby Lake Constance. Wohnen am Park residential development, Saurer WerkZwei site, Arbon, invited competition project, HRS Real Estate AG: 2013.

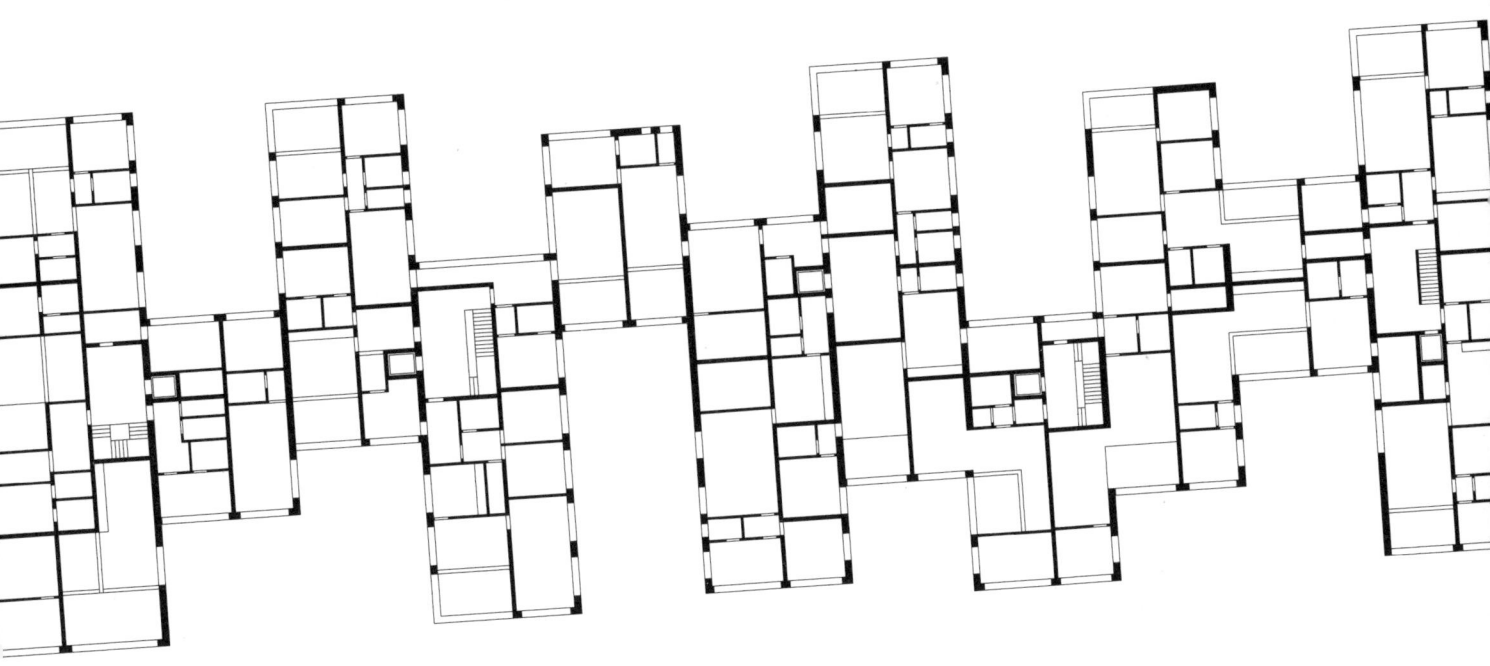

In Ägypten wurde um 1300 v. Chr. der Dreistreifen-Grundriss entwickelt. Die einzelnen Bereiche umfassten die Vorhalle, die Mittelhalle und die privaten Wohn- sowie die Wirtschaftsräume. Haus in Amarna, Mittelägypten.

House in Amarna, Middle Egypt. The tripartite floor plan evolved in Egypt in approx. 1300 BC. The individual areas included the vestibule hall, central hall, and area with the living quarters, as well as the utility spaces.

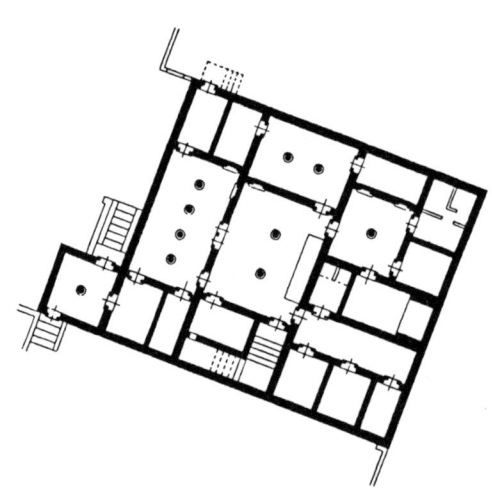

Die Einführung des Peristyls führte zu einer räumlichen Hierarchisierung des Hofes: Die gedeckten Umgänge haben etwas Korridorartiges und bilden einen Filter zur freien Mitte. Rekonstruktion einer Insula mit drei Hofhäusern. Rhodos, um 400 v. Chr.

Reconstruction of an insula with three courtyard houses (Rhodes, approx. 400 BC). The introduction of the peristyle led to a spatial hierarchization of the courtyard: the covered walkways have a corridor-like quality and form a filter to the open center.

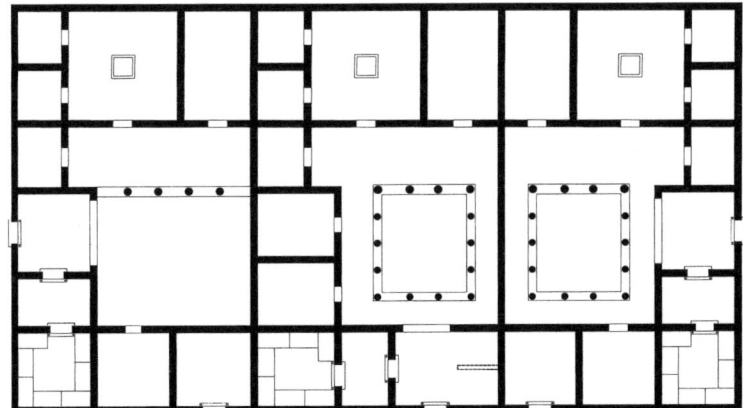

Der hallenartig angelegte und gespiegelt konzipierte Grundriss dieses Basler Schulhauses betont die Gleichwertigkeit aller Teile. Die Klassenzimmer legen sich dabei als Kammern an die raumhoch verglasten Fassaden. Mit der bewussten Vereinfachung der Raumanlage vermeidet der Bau eine Hierarchisierung seiner einzelnen Elemente. Orientierungsschule Kaltbrunnen (heute Primarschule Neubad), Basel, mit Jean-Pierre Wymann, Wettbewerb auf Einladung, Kanton Basel-Stadt: 1993; Fertigstellung Neubau: 1996.

The hall-like and duplicated concept of the ground plan of this Basel school emphasizes the equality of all the parts. Along the façades, which are glazed from floor to ceiling, the classrooms are laid out as chambers. Through the deliberate simplification of the spatial layout, the building avoids any hierarchy among the individual elements. Kaltbrunnen Secondary School (now Neubad Primary School), Basel, invited competition with Jean-Pierre Wymann, Canton Basel-Stadt: 1993; completion of new building: 1996.

↓ →

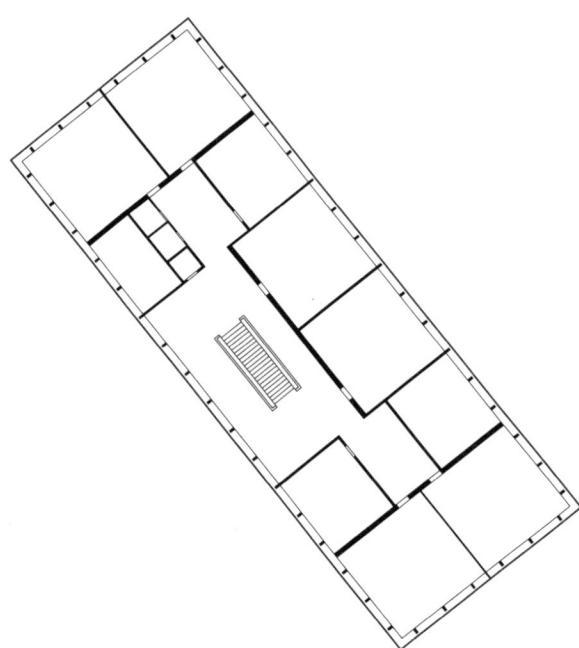

12

Serifen sind Ein- oder Zweiraumhäuser, gebildet aus Schilfbündeln und Schilfmatten, die seit dem 4. Jahrtausend v. Chr. bekannt waren. Darstellung einer Serife aus al Qurna (Irak).

Depiction of a *sarifa* from Al-Qurnah (present-day Iraq). Formed from bundles and woven mats of reeds, *sarifas* are one- or two-room houses which have been known to exist since the 4th millennium BC.

Über Raum und Räume

Regarding Space and Spaces

Luca Selva

In einer der ersten Vorlesungen meines Architekturstudiums an der ETH Lausanne referierte der Professor über Louis I. Kahn und dessen *espaces servis et espaces servants*. Ich erinnere mich noch ganz genau, wie sich damals Widerstand in mir regte. Zwar verstand ich sehr wohl, dass in Kahns Architektur mit der Inszenierung des grossen zentralen Raumes alle weiteren Räume zu versteckten Dienstleistern werden müssen. Trotzdem konnte ich mich dem Glauben an den einen grossen Raum nicht anschliessen. In den Anfängen meines Studiums in den ausgehenden 1980er-Jahren wurde beispielsweise anhand der Architektur von Mario Botta diese Glorifizierung zentraler Räume — diese Einheit des Raumes — intensiv diskutiert.

Wenn ich an die Architektur von Louis I. Kahn dachte, so war mir das parataktische Prinzip des Kimbell Art Museum in Fort Worth viel näher →1. Hier sind es gleiche Räume in einer parallelen Komposition mit präzisen

In one of the first lectures I heard during my architectural studies at the Swiss Federal Institute of Technology in Lausanne, the professor spoke about Louis I. Kahn and his *served and servant spaces.* I still remember quite distinctly how this provoked resistance in me at that time. Although I very much understood that with his staging of a large central space, in Kahn's architecture all other spaces had to become hidden service providers, nevertheless I personally failed to subscribe to this belief in a sole large space. At the beginning of my studies in the late 1980s, this glorification of central spaces—this unity of space—was discussed intensively, based on the architecture, for instance, of Mario Botta.

Auslassungen, Repetitionen von gleichen oder ähnlichen Räumen, *same but different*, die differenziert wahrgenommen werden können. Der Fokus liegt nicht auf dem einzig kostbaren und erhabenen Raum, er liegt vielmehr auf der Gesamtheit des Raumes, der sich aus vielen Teilen fügt, wo Gleiches unterschiedlich und damit räumlich herausfordernd wird. Dieses Vertrauen in die Kraft des Einfachen, das mich auch an den bildkünstlerischen Arbeiten von Donald Judd, Carl André oder in der Musik von Philip Glass faszinierte, hat mich im Denken über Architektur begleitet. Schon beim Wettbewerb für das Kaltbrunnen-Schulhaus in Basel→12, den ich kurz nach meinem Studium zusammen mit Jean-Pierre Wymann gewonnen hatte, galt die Recherche der möglichst einfachen Teilung des Raumes oder der Suche nach der kanonischen Form, mit dem Ziel einer selbstverständlichen Würde der einzelnen Räume, die gemeinsam Raum bilden.

Wenn wir im vorliegenden Band über Raum und Räume nachdenken, so hat dies mit der permanenten Recherche unseres Büros zu diesen Fragestellungen zu tun. Wir haben uns intensiv mit den Prinzipien von gleichwertigen zellenartigen und verbundenen Räumen beschäftigt und dabei Themen der *Kammerung* untersucht. In vielen Projekten haben wir diese einfachen und doch so reichen Raumbildungen erfolgreich eingesetzt und konnten in Aarburg →57 zum ersten Mal ein solches Raumkonzept in grösserem Massstab verwirklichen. Weitere Häuser im Baumwoll-Quartier in Köln werden folgen →58–61. In diesem von uns entwickelten städtebaulichen Plan, in dem Neubauten die scheinbar zufällig gesetzten denkmalgeschützten Hallengebäude zu einem neuen Ganzen führen, muss sich die Architektur der Neubauten an anerkannten Denkmälern messen lassen. Im Sinne einer Verwandtschaft der Raumbildung haben wir eine Vielzahl der Neubauten aus dem Prinzip der unhierarchischen Kammerung der

When I thought about the architecture of Kahn, however, the paratactic principle of the Kimbell Art Museum in Fort Worth was far more appealing to me →1. Here the spaces are equal, arranged in a parallel composition with precise omissions, repetitions of the same or similar spaces—the *same but different*, which can be perceived distinctively. Attention is focused not on the one and only precious and grand space, but instead far more on the space as a whole, which is composed of many parts, where sameness becomes diversity and thereby becomes challenging spatially. This trust in the power of the simple, which also fascinated me in the artworks of Donald Judd and Carl André or in the music of Philip Glass, has guided me in my thinking about architecture. Already in the competition for the Kaltbrunnen Schoolhouse in Basel →12, which I won with Jean-Pierre Wymann shortly after finishing my studies, the inquiry was about exploring the simplest possible division of the space or the search for a canonical form with the aim of creating a natural dignity of the individual rooms that coalesce to form space.

The reflections about space and rooms contained in this volume mirror our firm's continual research into this question. We have concentrated intensively on the principles of equivalent cell-like and connected spaces, and in the process explored the themes and aspects of *chambering*. We have successfully incorporated the resulting simple but nevertheless extremely rich way of forming space into numerous projects, and were able to realize this specific spatial concept for the first time on a larger scale in Aarburg →57. Further residential buildings will follow in the Baumwoll-Quartier residential development in Cologne, embedded in an urban development plan that we ourselves evolved →58–61. The new buildings mold the seemingly randomly placed protected historic hall buildings into a new whole, whereby the architecture of the new buildings consciously asks to be measured against that of the recognized landmark monuments. In the sense of

Grundrisse heraus entwickelt, die sich als Replik auf die Grundrisse der bestehenden Hallen versteht.

Im Anschluss an das Aarburger Projekt war es unserem Büro ein Anliegen, diese Recherche in einer Publikation zusammenzutragen. Im Gespräch mit Christoph Wieser entstand die Idee, über die Dokumentation der eigenen Arbeit hinaus das Thema der Kammergrundrisse zu vertiefen. Wir waren erstaunt, dass über dieses unhierarchische Ordnungsprinzip noch kaum geforscht wurde. Vor diesem Hintergrund ist der präzise Essay von Christoph Wieser in diesem Band wohl einer der ersten Texte, der das Thema der gekammerten Räume in dieser Tiefe analysiert. So wurde aus der geplanten Publikation eine weiterführende Recherche, die wir in die Architekturdiskussion einbringen wollen und für die wir Parks Books als Verlag und Tilo Richter als weiteren Herausgeber gewinnen konnten. Das Gespräch mit Patrick Gmür fokussiert auf die Bedeutung von Kammergrundrissen in der täglichen Arbeit als Architektin oder Architekt und zeigt die Relevanz der Fragestellung. Valeria Bonin und Diego Bontognali von Bonbon haben erneut eine präzise grafische Umsetzung des Themas entwickelt; Anic Aklin unterstützte die Arbeit umsichtig von unserer Seite. Allen ganz herzlichen Dank dafür.

Zusammen mit David Gschwind, Roger Braccini und Sonja Christen haben wir diese architektonische Recherche über lange Jahre im Büro entwickelt, viele Kolleginnen und Kollegen in unserem Büro haben mit ihrer Neugierde und ihrer architektonischen Inspiration Wesentliches beigetragen. Die Recherche über Raum und Räume ist dank der Leidenschaft aller zu einem wichtigen Teil der Bürobiografie geworden. Und sie wird es wohl auch bleiben, denn es gibt noch viel zu entdecken.

a kinship in spatial modulation, what we undertook was to develop a large number of new buildings based on the principle of a non-hierarchical chambering of the floor plans, deliberately conceived as replicas of the floor plans of the existing halls.

Following the project in Aarburg, our office considered it important to compile this research in a publication. In conversation with Christoph Wieser, the idea arose to go beyond the documentation of our own work and to deepen the focus on the issue of chambered floor plans. We were amazed to discover that hardly any research has been conducted into this non-hierarchical principle of organization. Set against this background, the concise essay by Christoph Wieser in this volume is probably one of the first texts to analyze the subject of chambered spaces so thoroughly. So it was that the originally planned publication turned into an exercise in further research that we would now like to introduce into the architecture discourse, and for which we have been able to bring in Parks Books as publisher and Tilo Richter as additional editor. The exchange with Patrick Gmür focuses on the significance of chambered floor plans in the everyday work of an architect and demonstrates the relevance of the issue. Valeria Bonin and Diego Bontognali from Bonbon have once again developed a precise graphic rendering of the theme; Anic Aklin has prudently supported the work on our side. Many thanks to everyone for their commitment.

Together with David Gschwind, Roger Braccini, and Sonja Christen, we have developed this architectural research over many years in the firm, while numerous other colleagues in our office have contributed substantially with their curiosity and architectural inspiration. Thanks to the passion of all, this research regarding space and spaces has become an important part of the life story of the office. And it will probably stay that way, because there is still much to discover.

Archäologische Funde von Pfahlbauten an der Mozartstrasse in Zürich (um 1500 v. Chr.). Durch das Zusammenrücken der Einraumhäuser entstanden schmale Gassen und Kammern.

    Archaeological finds from pile dwellings on Mozartstrasse in Zurich (approx. 1500 BC). By moving the one-room houses closely together, narrow alleys and chambers were created.

↓

Für den Ersatzneubau einer Sekundarschule in Basel soll ein nach oben verjüngter, über fünf Schichten angelegter und terrassierter Baukörper entstehen, der sich zur nahen Autobahn hin verschlossen, zum eigenen Innenhof offen zeigt. Durch die Verlegung der Fluchtwege auf die Terrassen konnten die Hallen im Innern freigespielt werden. Sekundarschule Sandgruben, Basel, Projektwettbewerb im selektiven Verfahren, Kanton Basel-Stadt: 2012.

    The proposal for the new replacement secondary school in Basel is tapered towards the top, laid out over five tiers, and has a terraced architectural volume. The façade towards the nearby freeway is closed, while the building opens up to its own inner courtyard. By shifting the obligatory fire escape routes to the terraces, scope is given to freely determine the use of the interior halls. Sandgruben Secondary School, Basel, selective competition project entry, Canton Basel-Stadt: 2012.

→ →

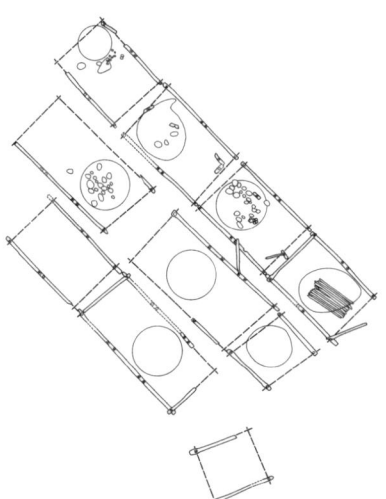

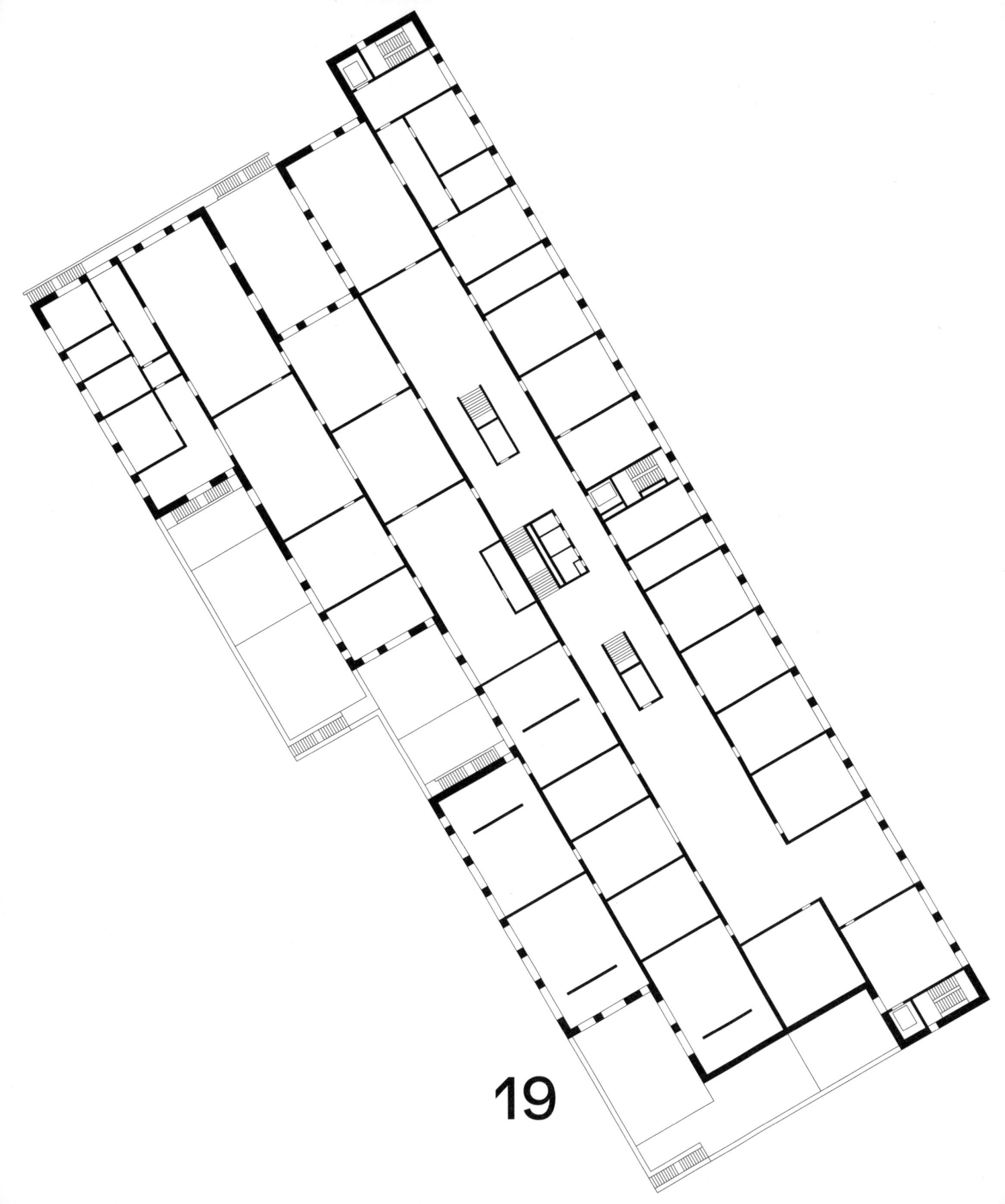
19

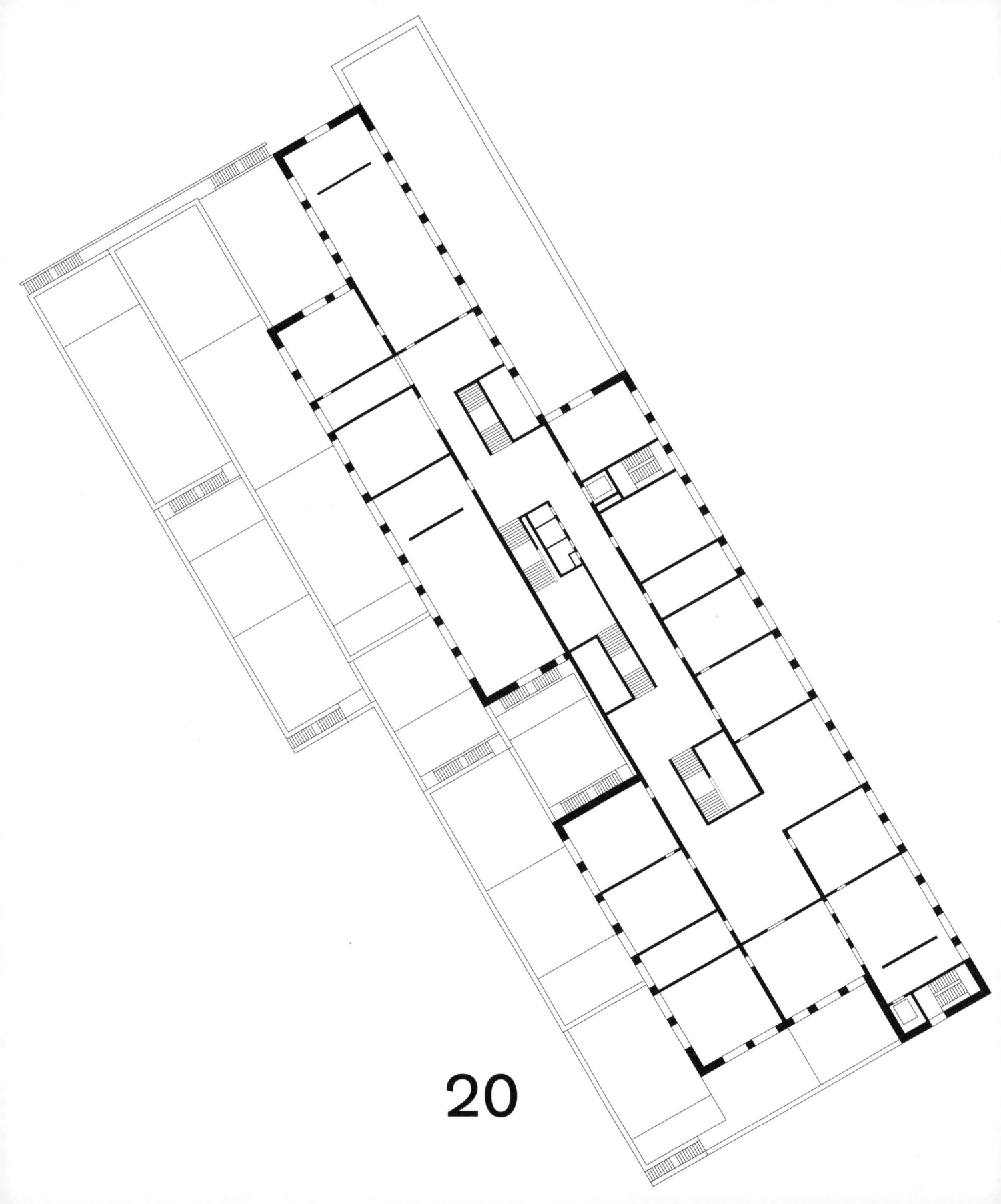

Bei Strickbauten sind die Zimmergrössen auf die Tragfähigkeit des Holzes abgestimmt. Durch Addition entsteht ein Kammergrundriss. Doppelhaus in Obermutten (Graubünden) mit dreiraumtiefen Wohngeschossen.

    Double-house in Obermutten (Graubünden) with three-room-deep living levels. In *Strickbauten* ("knitted" log buildings), the room size is tailored to the load-bearing capacity of wood. By adding onto the building, a chambered floor plan is created.

    ↓

Als «Passstück im Quartier» fügt sich das komplexe Bauvolumen dieser Primarschule in ein städtisches Transformationsgebiet ein. Auf einem ehemaligen Bahnareal und in unmittelbarer Nachbarschaft zur historischen und neuen Blockrandbebauung entstand ein Gebäude für zwölf Regelklassen, das die Baugesetze raumplastisch abbildet. Auf acht Geschossen sind bis zu fünf Raumschichten nebeneinandergefügt. Primarschule Erlenmatt, Basel, Projektwettbewerb im offenen Verfahren, Kanton Basel-Stadt: 2012; Fertigstellung: 2017.

    Conceived as a "fitted piece for the quarter," the complex architectural volume of this primary school accommodates the particular situation of an urban area undergoing transformation. Located on a former railroad freight yard in the immediate vicinity of historical and new perimeter housing blocks, a structure housing twelve standard classrooms was created that manifests the building regulations in a spatial-sculptural form. Up to five spatial layers are arranged side by side on eight floors. Erlenmatt Primary Schoolhouse, Basel, open project competition, Canton Basel-Stadt: 2012; completion: 2017.

    → →

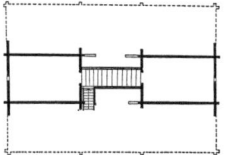

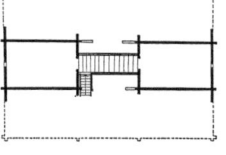

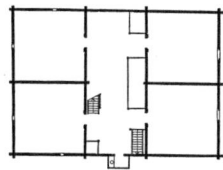

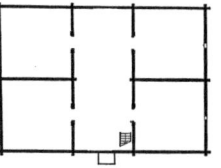

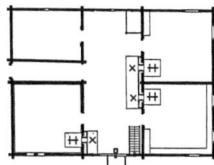

23

Beim norddeutschen Dielen- oder Hallenhaus ist das Prinzip subtraktiv: In den Grossraum wurden je nach Bedarf unterschiedlich viele und unterschiedlich dimensionierte Kammern eingebaut. Grundriss eines Bauernhauses in Westfalen.

Floor plan of a farmhouse in Westphalia. In the *Dielenhaus* (hallway house) or *Hallenhaus* (hall house) in northern Germany, the principle is subtractive: depending on need, a different number of variously dimensioned chambers were built in the large space.

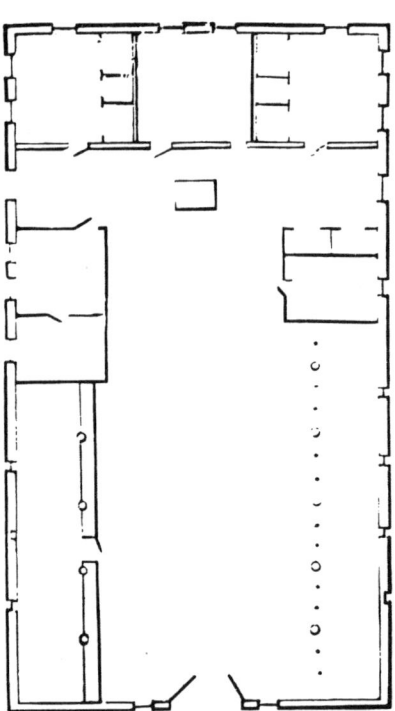

Das traditionelle Engadinerhaus weist keine Korridore auf und ist als «Einhof» ausgebildet: Die Wohn- und Wirtschaftsräume, Stall und Scheune liegen alle unter einem Dach. Schema einer idealtypischen Verteilung.

Generalized scheme of the typical spatial distribution in a traditional Engadine house. Designed as an *Einhof* (all-in-one farmhouse) with no corridors, the living quarters and utility areas, including the stable and barn, are all under one roof.

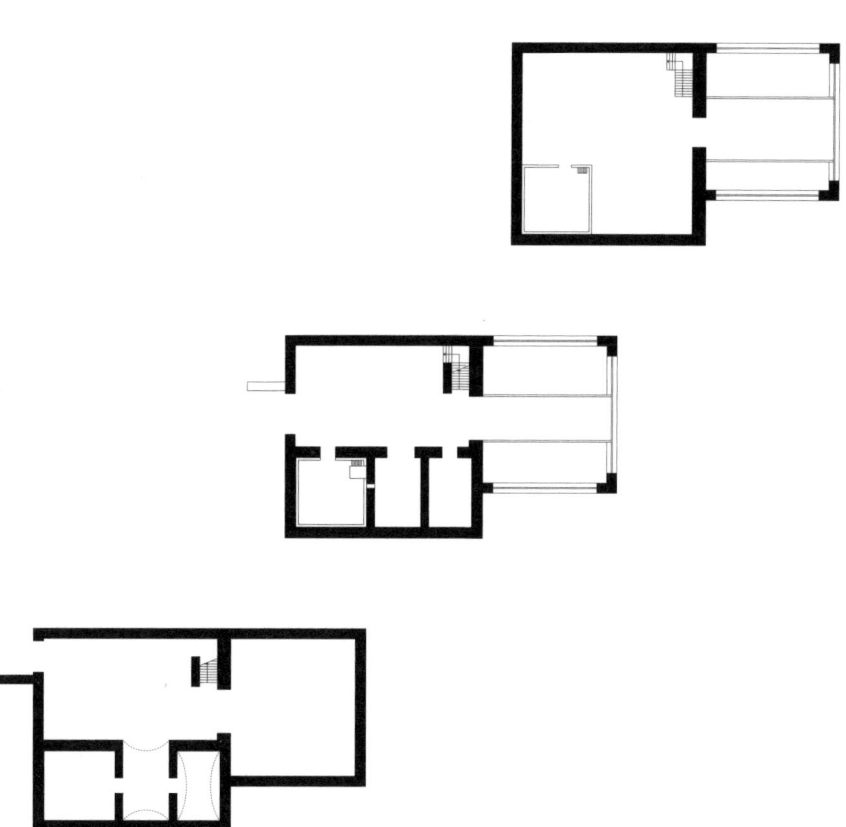

Luca Selva Architekten stapeln hier das Raumprogramm vertikal. Die Nutzung eines Punkthochhauses teilt sich in Wohnungen, Hotel und Büros, die mit unterschiedlichen Volumen die Gesamtform bilden. In Wohnetagen, wie der hier gezeigten, sind die Grundrisse so organisiert, dass sich hinter den gläsernen Fassaden umlaufend zwei bis drei gekammerte Raumschichten entwickeln. Tower in Brugg-Windisch, Studienauftrag auf Einladung, Brugg Immobilien AG: 2013.

In this project, Luca Selva Architekten have vertically stacked the spatial program. The usage within the solitary high-rise is divided into apartments, a hotel, and offices, which are accommodated within different volumes that together constitute the overall form. On the residential floors, like the one shown here, the floor plans have been developed in two- to three-chambered spatial layers around the entire periphery of the building. Tower in Brugg-Windisch, invited study commission, Brugg Immobilien AG: 2013.

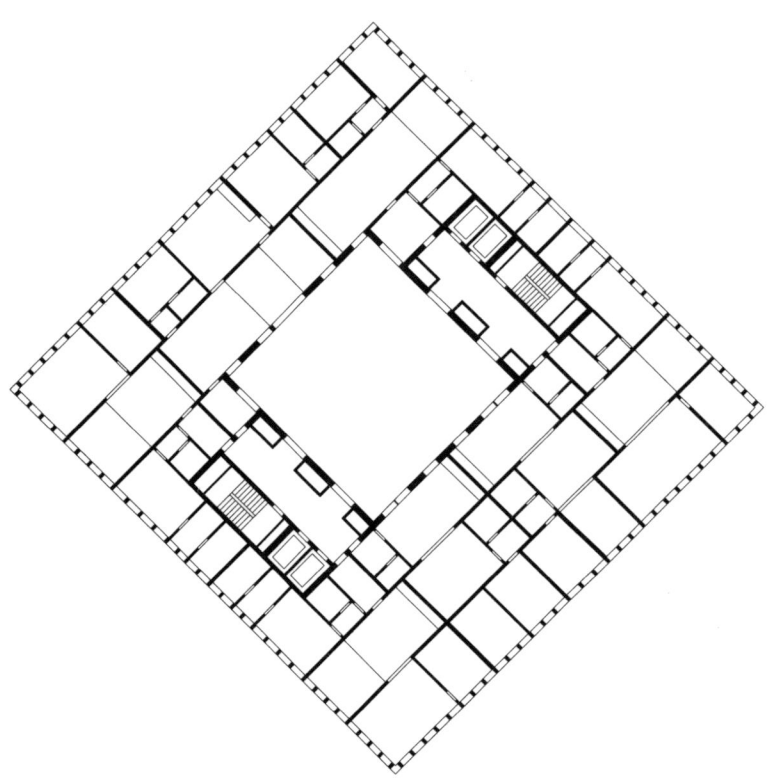

Sogenannter Schustertyp: Das Treppenhaus erschliesst je zwei Schulzimmer pro Geschoss. Dadurch können sie zweiseitig belichtet werden und verfügen über hallenartige Vorräume, hier gezeigt am Beispiel eines Entwurfs von Alfred Roth, 1932.

Design concept (1932) by Alfred Roth as an example of the "Schuster type" layout. The staircase serves two classrooms per level, a solution that gives them daylight exposure on two sides and provides a hall-like anteroom.

↓

Räumliche Spannung entsteht bei der Hallenschule durch die unterschiedlichen Dimensionen von Aufenthaltsbereichen und Unterrichtsräumen. Kleine Höfe ermöglichen die Belichtung hintereinandergeschalteter Räume. Bundesschulzentrum in Wörgl von Viktor Hufnagl und Fritz Gerhard Mayer mit modularem Grundriss, 1973.

Bundesschulzentrum in Wörgl (1973) by Viktor Hufnagl and Fritz Gerhard Mayr with a modular floor plan. Spatial tension results in the so-called "hall school" type through the different dimensions of amenity spaces and classrooms. Small courtyards make it possible to ensure spaces connected in series are all exposed to daylight.

→

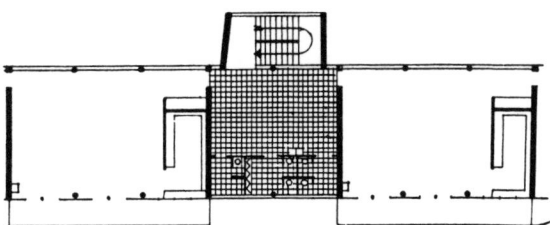

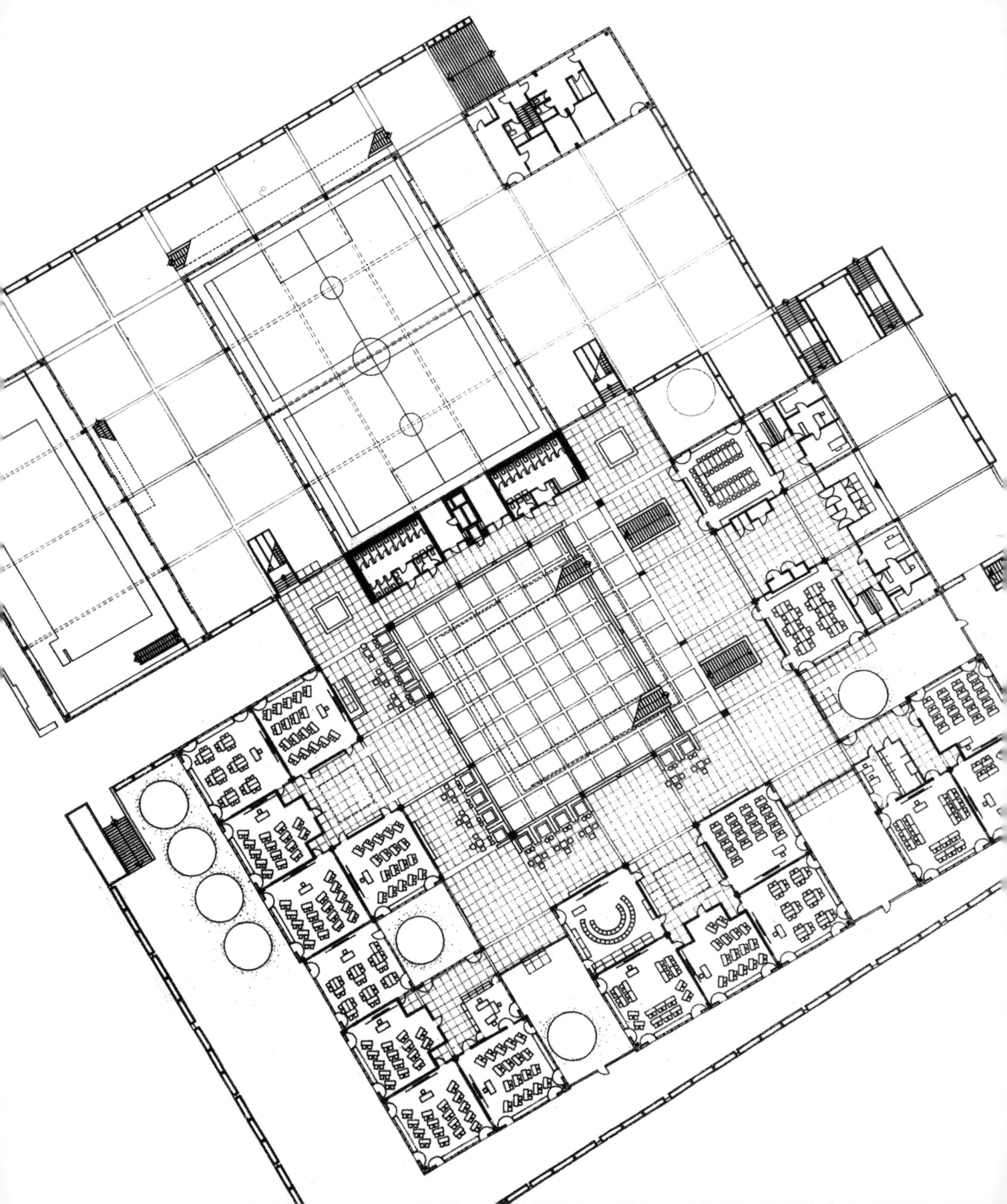

Vielfalt in der Einheit

Variety in Unity

Christoph Wieser

Betrachtungen zum Kammergrundriss

Reflections on the Chambered Floor Plan

Ein Grundriss, gebildet aus lauter einzelnen, gefassten Räumen. Ohne Korridor. Verbindungen gibt es dort, wo Durchgänge und Blickachsen erwünscht sind. Trotz einfacher, zellenartiger Struktur sind die Möglichkeiten zur Erzeugung räumlicher Komplexität sowie zum differenzierten Zusammenspiel der Kammern gross. Dieses elementare, unhierarchische Ordnungsprinzip spielt seit jeher eine zentrale Rolle in der Entwicklung der verschiedensten Grundrisstypologien, von der einfachsten Hütte bis zum vielgestaltigen Museum. Immer wieder fasziniert der Gegensatz zwischen stempelartiger Einfachheit des Plans und einer überraschenden Vielfältigkeit im tatsächlichen Erleben solcher Raumgefüge. Umso erstaunlicher, dass der Kammer- oder

A floor plan, formed out of nothing but individual, enclosed spaces. Without corridors. Connections exist where passageways and lines of sight are desired. Despite the simple, cell-like structure, there are many possibilities for creating both spatial complexity and a differentiated interplay of the chambered units. This elementary, non-hierarchical compositional principle has played a central role in the development of a diverse range of floor plan typologies, from the simplest hut to the multiform museum.

Zellengrundriss, wie er auch genannt wird, in der Literatur bislang kaum vertieft behandelt worden ist.[1]

Im Werk von Luca Selva Architekten bildet der Kammergrundriss ein eigenständiges Forschungsfeld innerhalb ihrer entwerferischen Tätigkeit. Er dient — unabhängig von der Bauaufgabe — als Mittel, um über grundlegende architektonische Fragen nachzudenken, etwa über die räumliche Aufteilung, Zuordnung und Effizienz sowie die Gliederung und Hierarchisierung im Kleinen wie im Grossen. Bereits beim Kaltbrunnen-Schulhaus in Basel (1993–1996) → 12, das noch in Arbeitsgemeinschaft mit Jean-Pierre Wymann entstand, lassen sich Anklänge an einen Kammergrundriss erkennen. Im Lauf der Jahre kam eine Reihe weiterer Bauten und Projekte hinzu, die sich auf unterschiedliche und differenzierte Weise mit diesem Thema auseinandersetzten. Ein wesentlicher Reiz — möglicherweise auch Antrieb — für die fortgesetzte Suche liegt in der scheinbaren Einfachheit dieses Grundrissprinzips, das in Tat und Wahrheit grosse Herausforderungen stellt: Einer mathematischen Gleichung mit mehreren Variablen ähnlich, gilt es alle Ansprüche so aufeinander abzustimmen, dass am Schluss ein räumlicher Aufbau entsteht, der strukturell ebenso einfach wie funktional überzeugend ist.

Denn die Logik der Kammerung schafft zunächst einmal Zwänge, die in Vorteile überführt werden müssen. Erst dann ist die Strategie erfolgreich. Das erfuhren die Architekten beim Wettbewerb für die Wohnüberbauung Sandfelsen → 6 in Erlenbach (2009), als sie zum ersten Mal einen reinen Kammergrundriss im Wohnungsbau vorschlugen. Allein, die Wohnungen waren noch zu gross, die Flächen und funktionalen Zuordnungen zu wenig optimiert, als dass eine ökonomisch tragfähige Lösung entstanden wäre. Das Interesse für diese Art von Kombinatorik war jedoch geweckt.

Im Folgenden sollen Entwicklungslinien und charakteristische Merkmale des Kammergrundrisses

The contrast between the compartmental simplicity of the plan and the surprising variation in the actual lived experience of such spatial structures is always fascinating. Therefore, it is all the more astonishing that the chambered floor plan, or cellular floor plan as it is sometimes also called, has so far hardly been discussed in depth in the literature.[1]

Considering the body of work of Luca Selva Architekten, the chambered floor plan constitutes an independent field of research within their design practice. It serves—regardless of the requirements of the projected building—as a means of reflecting on fundamental architectural concerns, such as division, allocation, and efficiency of spaces, as well as structuring and hierarchization on both small and large scales. Already in the Kaltbrunnen Schoolhouse in Basel (1993–1996) → 12, which was co-realized with Jean-Pierre Wymann, echoes of a chambered floor plan can be recognized. Over the years a series of other buildings and projects have followed that deal with this theme in different and differentiated ways. A key trigger—possibly also the underlying drive—sparking the ongoing search lies in the apparent simplicity of this floor plan principle, which in fact poses great challenges: like a mathematical equation with several variables, all the demands have to be coordinated with one another so that the ultimate spatial composition is both structurally simple and functionally convincing.

This is because the logic of chambering initially creates constraints that have to be converted into advantages. Only then can the strategy be successful. This is something that the architects learned with the competition for the Sandfelsen housing development → 6 in Erlenbach (2009) when they proposed an entirely chambered floor plan for a residential building for the first time. However, the apartments were still too big and the surface area and functional allocation too little optimized for the proposal to be an economically viable solution. Nevertheless, an interest in this type of combinatorics was kindled.

als historischer und theoretischer Hintergrund mit der Reflexion über ausgewählte Bauten und Projekte von Luca Selva Architekten verbunden werden. Dabei zeigt sich eine erstaunliche Wandelbarkeit sowie Permanenz dieser ursprünglichen Bauweise: Seitdem der Mensch sesshaft geworden ist und sich das Bauen von rechteckigen Häusern aus naheliegenden Gründen durchsetzen konnte, galt der Kammergrundriss bis Anfang des 18. Jahrhunderts für die meisten Bauaufgaben als Normalfall.[2]

Erst mit dem Aufkommen des Bürgertums, das zu einer völlig neuen Form des Zusammenlebens führte und die Privatsphäre zu einem wichtigen Gut erklärte, etablierte sich der Korridor als typologisches Element, von dem aus die einzelnen Zimmer direkt betreten werden.[3] Heute finden sich je nach Bauaufgabe und entwerferischen Absichten beide Lösungsansätze nebeneinander: Bei Hotels, Flughafen-Terminals, Krankenhäusern und Gefängnissen beispielsweise drängen sich Korridore auf; bei Wohnbauten, Schulhäusern und Museen dagegen stellen Kammergrundrisse weiterhin gute Alternativen dar.

Zellularer Massivbau

Zu den sehr frühen Ansammlungen von rechteckigen Häusern zählt die Siedlung Çatal Höyük →2 in Anatolien (Türkei), die um 7000 v. Chr. aus getrockneten Lehmziegeln erbaut wurde.[4] Jedes Haus bestand aus einem Raum, der über Niveauunterschiede des Bodens in unterschiedliche Zonen gegliedert war. Die Häuser standen Mauer an Mauer und wurden über eine Luke im Dach betreten und belüftet.[5] Die Auslagerung der Erschliessung auf die Dächer ermöglichte eine unglaublich kompakte Anlage, die als Ganzes wie ein grosser Kammergrundriss wirkt, dessen Zellen untereinander jedoch nicht verbunden waren.

Eine erste Weiterentwicklung, und damit die Etablierung eines Kammergrundrisses im eigentlichen Sinn, stellen die Mittelsaal- und Hofhäuser dar, die

In what follows, lines of development and characteristic features of the chambered floor plan as a historical and theoretical background will be combined with reflections on selected buildings and projects by Luca Selva Architekten. What emerges is the astonishing versatility as well as the permanence of this primordial architectural approach: ever since humans became sedentary and the erection of rectangular buildings, for obvious reasons, became prevalent, the chambered floor plan was considered the norm for meeting the requirements of most projected buildings until the beginning of the 18th century.[2]

Only with the emergence of a commercial bourgeoisie—which led to a completely new form of shared living and proclaimed privacy to be a key commodity—did the corridor become established as a typological element from which the separate rooms could be directly entered.[3] Today, depending on the requirements of the projected building and the design intentions, both approaches can be found side by side: in hotels, airport terminals, hospitals, and prisons, for instance, the advantages of corridors are self-evident; while, in contrast, for residential buildings, schoolhouses, and museums, chambered floor plans continue to represent good alternatives.

Cellular Solid Construction

Çatalhöyük →2 in Anatolia in Turkey, built around 7000 BC from dried loam bricks, is considered to be one of the earliest settlements of rectangular houses.[4] Each house consisted of a space that was subdivided into different zones by variations in the floor level. The houses stood wall-to-wall and were entered and ventilated through a hatch or port in the roof.[5] Direct access to the roofs made an incredibly compact system possible, which as a whole seems like a huge chambered floor plan, but whose individual cells are not interconnected with one another.

Die tragende Betonkonstruktion erzeugt im Innern einen Kammergrundriss und ist in den Fassaden als Skelettstruktur ablesbar. Haus in Tavole von Herzog & de Meuron, 1988.

Stone House (1988), Tavole, by Herzog & de Meuron. The load-bearing concrete structure creates a chambered floor plan in the interior and is recognizable on the façade through the visible outlines of the exposed skeletal structure.

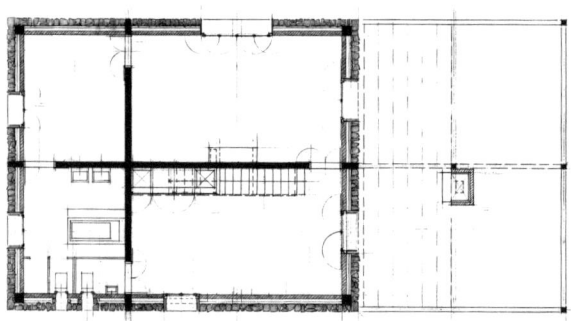

um 3500 v. Chr. von der Uruk-Kultur im heutigen Syrien hervorgebracht wurden.[6] Das Prinzip ist bei beiden Typen dasselbe: Von einem zentralen Verteilraum aus, sei es ein Saal oder ein Hof, wurden die Räume erschlossen → 3/7. Die Häuser waren oft ohne Abstand zueinander gebaut, sodass die Belüftung und Belichtung nicht über die Seitenfassaden, sondern über den Hof oder Öffnungen im oberen Bereich des überhöhten Saals gewährleistet werden mussten.

Mit der zunehmenden Grösse der privaten Wohnbauten stieg die Komplexität der Grundrisse. Im alten Ägypten kam um 1300 v. Chr. das sogenannte Dreistreifen-Haus auf, das im Wesentlichen aus drei in der Tiefe gestaffelten Raumschichten bestand → 10, der Vorhalle, der Haupthalle und den privaten Wohn- und Wirtschaftskammern.[7] Auch bei dieser Weiterentwicklung des Mittelsaalhauses gab es keine Korridore, sondern die Hallen dienten als Aufenthalts- und Verteilräume und sorgten ebenfalls mittels hoch liegender Öffnungen für ausreichend Licht und Luft. Aus Gründen der Belichtung weisen die wenigsten Kammergrundrisse mehr als drei Streifen auf, ausser sie verfügen über Oberlichter. Bei Luca Selva Architekten gibt es zwar Projekte mit sechs Schichten — etwa beim Entwurf für das ehemalige Baumwoll-Quartier in Köln (2016–2020) —, die einzelnen Wohnungen sind aber nur maximal vier Räume tief und auch nur dann, wenn sie zweiseitig belichtet sind → 58.

Das Hofhaus wiederum erhielt mit der Einführung eines Peristyls, das heisst eines säulenumstandenen Hofs wie in Rhodos um 400 v. Chr.[8], eine wesentliche Änderung: Der zentrale Verteiler trat zwar aufgrund der Durchlässigkeit zwischen den Säulen weiterhin als zusammenhängender Raum in Erscheinung, erhielt im Bereich der lateralen Umgänge jedoch bereits einen korridorartigen Charakter. Gleichwohl blieb bei diesem Grundrisstyp die Kammerung das vorherrschende Prinzip → 11.

The first refinements—which, strictly speaking, mark the actual establishment of the chambered floor plan—were the middle room house and the courtyard house, which originated around 3500 BC with the Uruk culture in present-day Syria.[6] The principle is the same for both types: the spaces were accessible via a central distribution space, be it a hall or courtyard → 3/7. The houses were often built without a gap between them, so that ventilation and daylight were not provided through the side façades but rather through the courtyard or openings in the upper area of the vertically extended hall.

As private residential buildings became larger, the floor plans became more complex. In ancient Egypt around 1300 BC the so-called tripartite plan house → 10 emerged, which essentially consisted of three spatial layers staggered in depth: the vestibule hall, the main hall, and the private living quarters and chambers, together with the utility rooms.[7] This refinement of the middle room house likewise dispensed with corridors, the halls instead serving as amenity and node areas, at the same time guaranteeing sufficient daylighting and ventilation, provided through openings at the top of the high walls. In order to ensure proper light, very few chambered floor plans feature more than three layers except where they have roof lights. At Luca Selva Architekten, there are projects with six layers—for instance in the design concept for the Baumwoll-Quartier in Cologne (2013–2020)—but the individual apartments are only a maximum of four rooms deep, and only then if daylit from both sides → 58.

On the other hand, with the introduction of the peristyle—in other words a courtyard surrounded by a row of columns, as for example in Rhodes in around 400 BC[8]—the courtyard house underwent a major change: while the central distribution node continued to exist as a contiguous space owing to the permeability between the columns, it already acquired a corridor-like character in the area of

Kammerung im Skelettbau

Die ersten Skelettbauten waren klein und wiesen in der Regel nur einen Raum auf: Seien es die sogenannten Serifen→14, die seit dem 4. Jahrtausend im heutigen Irak aus Schilfbündeln und Schilfmatten gebildet wurden,[9] oder die Häuser der Pfahlbauer. Spannend ist eine Ausgrabung von Pfahlbauten an der Mozartstrasse in Zürich→18, die auf 1500 v. Chr. datiert werden, da sie so eng beieinanderstehen, dass fast ein mehrschichtiger Kammergrundriss entsteht.[10]

Block- oder Strickbauten wurden schon früh als Mehrraum-Häuser mit oder ohne Korridor ausgeführt.[11] Bei dieser traditionellen Bauweise des Alpenraumes ist die Grösse der Kammern auf die Tragfähigkeit des Holzes abgestimmt→21. Mittels Verstrickung der Balken konnten zudem Kammern über die natürliche Stammlänge hinaus addiert werden.

Subtraktiv hingegen ist das Prinzip beim Dielen- und Hallenhaus→24, das in Norddeutschland seit dem 13. Jahrhundert verbreitet ist: Eine massive Ständerkonstruktion trägt ein grosses, schützendes Dach. In diesen Grossraum wurden entlang der Fassaden je nach Bedarf einzelne Kammern eingebaut, die direkt von der multifunktionalen Diele aus erschlossen waren.[12] Obwohl ein Massivbau, ist das typische Engadiner Bauernhaus→25 ähnlich konzipiert und wird als «Einhof» bezeichnet, weil die Wohn- und Wirtschaftsräume sowie der Stall und die Scheune ebenfalls unter einem Dach liegen.[13] Von der Halle im Erdgeschoss, dem Sulér, werden Stube, Küche und Vorratsraum direkt betreten; der vom Obergeschoss bis unters Dach reichende Raum (Palantschin) beherbergt die Schlafkammer, die aus klimatischen Gründen direkt über der Stube liegt.[14]

Die Kombination von Hallen und Stuben, das heisst von grossen und kleinen Räumen, ist typisch für Kammergrundrisse, weil sie dank dieser Gliederung viel flexibler genutzt werden können. Dabei dienen selbstredend die lateral ambulatories. Nevertheless, with this type of floor plan, chambering still remained the predominant principle→11.

Chambering in Framed Structures

The first framed buildings were small and usually featured only a single space—be it so-called *sarifas*→14, which have been formed from bundles and woven mats of reeds since the 4th millennium BC in what is now Iraq,[9] or the buildings of the pile dwellers. An excavation of pile dwellings on Mozartstrasse in Zurich→18, which date back to 1500 BC, is especially interesting because they are so close together that they almost form a multi-layered chambered floor plan.[10]

From early times, log buildings—known in Switzerland as *Strickbauten*, "knitted" timber buildings—were executed as multi-room houses with or without a corridor.[11] In the traditional Alpine construction method, the size of the chambers is tailored to the load-bearing capacity of the wood→21. By meshing the notched beams, it was also possible to add chambers that were longer than the natural length of the tree trunks.

On the other hand, the principle behind the timber-framed *Dielenhaus* (hallway house) and the *Hallenhaus* (hall house)→24, widespread in northern Germany since the 13th century, is subtractive: a solid post-and-beam construction supports a big protective roof. In this large space, individual chambers were inserted along the façades as required, which were directly accessible from the multifunctional *Diele* (hallway).[12] Although a solid construction, the typical Engadine farmhouse→25 is conceived in a similar way and is called an *Einhof* (an all-in-one farmhouse), because the residential spaces and even the utility areas, including the stable and barn, are likewise all under one roof.[13] The *Sulér*, the gateway hall on the ground floor, provides direct access to the *Stube* or traditional parlor,

grösseren Räume auch als Erschliessung der kleineren Zellen. Diese wiederum sind, je nach Gebrauch, teilweise untereinander verbunden, womit funktionale Einheiten entstehen. Die Anordnung und Anzahl der Durchgänge ist, das zeigt sich schon bei den frühesten Beispielen deutlich, ein wichtiges Mittel zum Aufbau von Kammergrundrissen. Mit solchen Massnahmen lassen sich die grundsätzlich unhierarchischen Strukturen je nach nutzungsbedingten Abläufen und räumlichen Vorstellungen differenziert regeln.

Schulhäuser

Schulhäuser sind bestes Beispiel dafür, wie Hallen und Zimmer zu einem komplexen Organismus gefügt werden können. Der Klassentrakt des Kaltbrunnen-Schulhauses→12 bezieht sich auf ein Schema, das vom anspruchslosen Dorfschulhaus bis zu den Palastschulhäusern des frühen 20. Jahrhunderts weit verbreitet war: Das Treppenhaus ist als Halle aufgefasst und bildet mit den horizontalen Erschliessungsflächen, die zu grosszügigen Aufenthaltsräumen ausgeweitet sind, eine Einheit. Hier befinden sich die Garderoben und die Türen zu den seitlich angegliederten Zimmern. In Abweichung von diesem, in der Regel symmetrisch aufgebauten Grundtyp schliessen sich beim Kaltbrunnen-Schulhaus an den Stirnseiten der Hallen noch kleinere Räume mit den Garderoben an. Dank dieser leichten Abgrenzung vom lärmigen Betrieb der öffentlichen Bereiche erhalten die Klassenzimmer eine räumlich gefasste und dennoch mit der Halle verbundene Vorzone von gutem Zuschnitt.

Eine vergleichbare Wirkung suchte Alfred Roth bei seinem Vorschlag für ein dreigeschossiges Schulhaus (1932)→27, bei dem jeweils zwei Unterrichtsräume von einer gemeinsamen Treppe bedient werden und über hallenartige Vorzonen verfügen.[15] Der Gewinn dieser schlanken Lösung liegt, wie er schreibt, in der zweiseitigen Belichtung der Schulzimmer und den Qualitäten der Verkehrsflächen:

the kitchen, and the pantry; the space extending from the upper floor up to the roof (the *Palantschin*) houses the bedchamber, which for climatic reasons lies directly above the *Stube*.[14]

The combination of halls and *Stuben*, in other words large and small spaces, is typical of chambered floor plans, because thanks to this subdivision they can be used much more flexibly. Of course, in this constellation the larger rooms also serve as circulation spaces for accessing smaller cells. In turn, and depending on their use, these smaller areas are partially connected to one another, creating functional units. As the earliest examples clearly show, the arrangement and number of passages are important means of creating chambered floor plans. With such measures, these fundamentally non-hierarchical structures can be patterned differentially according to their usage-related routines and spatial concepts.

Schoolhouses

Schoolhouses are the best examples of how halls and rooms can be joined to form a complex organism. The classroom wing of the Kaltbrunnen Schoolhouse→12 adopts the same schoolhouse scheme that was applied in the past, ranging from modest village types to the palace-like examples widespread up until the early 20th century. The staircase is conceived as a hall and forms one unit with the horizontal circulation areas that are enlarged into generous spaces for congregating and relaxing. This is where the cloakrooms and doors to the adjoining rooms arranged on the sides are located. Departing from this generally symmetrical basic type, the Kaltbrunnen Schoolhouse joins the even smaller spaces with cloakroom areas at the front sides of the halls. Thanks to this slight shielding from the noisy bustle of the common areas, the classrooms acquire an anteroom with a good layout, which is spatially framed yet still well connected to the hall.

Alfred Roth aimed to achieve a comparable effect in his proposal for

Gegenüberstellung der Prinzipien von Massiv- und Skelettbau. Le Corbusier illustrierte so seine *Fünf Punkte einer Neuen Architektur* (1927) und verwies damit auf die Unterschiede zwischen gekammerten und fliessenden Grundrissen.

Juxtaposition of the principles of solid and skeleton-frame construction. Through this contrast, Le Corbusier illustrated his "Five Points Towards a New Architecture" (1927), thereby referring to the differences between chambered and open flowing floor plans.

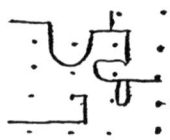

«Die ‹korridorlose› Lösung hat sogar den Vorteil, dass die Schüler automatisch in kleine Gruppen aufgeteilt werden, denen eigene Eingänge und Ausgänge nach dem Pausenplatz zur Verfügung stehen. Gleichzeitig bilden die eingeschobenen Hallen wertvolle, die Intimität des Hauses erhöhende räumliche Elemente und gestatten eine gute Lösung der Garderobenfrage.»[16]

Was die Dimensionen betrifft, ist der Kontrast zwischen den Aufenthaltsbereichen und den Schulzimmern in den sogenannten Hallenschulen am grössten, die in den 1960er-Jahren Konjunktur hatten. Dort dient die Treppenhalle als Aufenthalts- und Erschliessungsraum sowie als räumliches Zentrum der Schule. In einem Kranz darum herum sind die Zimmer angeordnet. Wegen der unterschiedlichen Grössenverhältnisse geht der Charakter eines Kammergrundrisses jedoch verloren.

Anders bei Schulhäusern aus derselben Zeit, die eher clusterartig organisiert sind und deshalb auf eine Repetition gleicher, gruppenbildender Einheiten setzen. Dieses Vorgehen ist zweifellos vom Strukturalismus beeinflusst, der aber in der Regel offene, flexibel nutzbare Raumgerüste stark determinierten Kammerungen vorzog.[17]

Eine Mischung aus grosser Hallenschule und kleinteiliger, modularer Struktur ist das Bundesschulzentrum in Wörgl, Tirol, von Viktor Hufnagl (1973). Das Gebäude ist auch deshalb interessant, weil hier der Versuch unternommen wurde, eine zweiraumtiefe Zimmerschicht um die Halle anzuordnen → 28. Das Belichtungsproblem, das sich bei Kammergrundrissen ab der zweiten Raumschicht immer einstellt, wurde hier über kleine Höfe und Vorhallen gelöst.[18]

Ebenfalls vielzellig aufgebaut ist die Primarschule Erlenmatt in Basel (2017) → 23. Sie ist das komplexeste Gebäude mit Kammerstruktur, das Luca Selva Architekten bislang bauen konnten. Das Schulhaus ist als sechsgeschossiges Volumen ausgebildet, das sich geschickt über mehrfache Abtreppungen und Rückstaffelungen in das

a three-story schoolhouse (1932) → 27, in which two classrooms are served by a common staircase and are equipped with hall-like antechamber zones.[15] The benefit of this streamlined solution lies, as he describes it, in the two-sided daylight exposure of the classrooms and the qualities of the circulation areas: "The elimination of corridors has the further advantage of automatically dividing the pupils into small groups with an independent access, exit and play space. The connecting stair-halls add, moreover, to the homey atmosphere of the school and afford an easy solution to the cloakroom problem."[16]

In terms of the dimensions, the contrast between the amenity spaces and the classrooms is greatest in the so-called *Hallenschulen* (hall-type schools), which were fashionable in the 1960s. There the staircase serves as amenity and circulation space, while simultaneously acting as the spatial center of the school. The rooms form a U-shaped wreath around this core space. Because of the different proportions, however, the character of a chambered floor plan is lost.

This is not the case with schoolhouses from the same period that are organized in a cluster-like manner and therefore rely on repetition of identical, group-forming units. This approach is undoubtedly influenced by Structuralism, which, however, as a rule preferred open, flexibly usable spaces created via spatial frames rather than highly articulated chambering.[17]

The Bundesschulzentrum (1973) in Wörgl, Tyrol, by Viktor Hufnagl is a mixture of a large hall-type school and a smaller, subdivided, more modular structure. The building is also interesting because an attempt was made to arrange a two-room-deep spatial layer around the hall → 28. Chambered floor plans present the inherent problem of channeling sufficient daylight into the second spatial layer and beyond, solved here by deploying small courtyards and anterooms.[18]

The Erlenmatt Primary Schoolhouse in Basel (2017) → 23 is likewise organized

dreieckige Grundstück einschreibt. Über die zu zwei Dritteln unterirdisch gelegene Turnhalle spannt sich das Tragwerk der Obergeschosse in einer strengen, parallel zur Eingangsfassade gelegten Struktur. Die bis zu acht Streifen weisen nahezu identische Tiefen auf und beherbergen nebst Kindergarten, Hort, Unterrichts- und Nebenräumen auch die innen liegende, immer wieder an die Fassade vorstossende Erschliessungsfigur. Mit ihren Richtungswechseln, Nischen und vertikalen Durchdringungen schafft sie einen räumlichen Gegenpol zur Kammerung der Schulzimmer und weiteren Nutzungen. Dabei ist sie so gestaltet, dass der durchgängige Rhythmus der Zellenstruktur jederzeit spürbar bleibt. Auch hier gibt es wenige zwei- oder gar dreiraumtiefe Bereiche (Hort). Aufgrund der vielgliedrigen Volumetrie profitieren jedoch etliche Räume von einer zweiseitigen Belichtung übereck.

Schottenbauweise als Mischform

Kammergrundrisse sind ihrem Wesen nach ungerichtet: Zwischen den Quer- und Längswänden gibt es strukturell gesehen keine Unterschiede. Beim Haus in Tavole von Herzog & de Meuron (1988) — zu dessen Entstehungszeit Luca Selva als Student dort im Büro arbeitete — ist dieses Kennzeichen gut sichtbar→32, teilt doch die kreuzförmige Betonstruktur das Gebäude in vier Räume, die über die Sichtbetonstützen in den Ansichten nachgezeichnet werden. Dementsprechend sind auch die Längs- und Stirnfassaden vom Prinzip her gleich gegliedert. Gerhard Mack schreibt dazu: «Es gibt keine dienenden Gänge und kein bewohnbares Zentrum. Die Räume stossen aneinander und fügen sich zu einem Gebilde zusammen, als wären vier Häuser von aussen zu einem Konglomerat gepresst worden und hätten dabei die Betonträger als Nähte zurückgelassen, an denen der Verschmelzungsprozess ablesbar bleibt.»[19]

Weil Kammergrundrissen keine bevorzugte Orientierung zu eigen ist, in a multi-cellular way. It is the most complex chamber-structured building that Luca Selva Architekten has had the opportunity to build to date. The schoolhouse is developed as a six-story volume, which is cleverly inscribed within the triangular plot via numerous terracings and setbacks. The load-bearing assemblage supporting the upper floors spans over the sports hall—which in turn is sunk up to two-thirds underground—in a strict structure situated parallel to the entrance façade. The up to eight spatial layers are almost identical in depth and house not only the kindergarten, after-school care facilities, classrooms, and ancillary areas, but also the interior circulation figure that repeatedly thrusts against the façade. Through changes of direction, niches, and vertical penetrations, this figure creates a spatial counterpoint to the chambering of the classrooms and other facilities. In the process, it is designed in such a way that the continuous rhythm of the cell structure can be sensed everywhere. Here, too, there are a small number of two- or even three-room-deep areas (the after-school care facilities). Nevertheless, owing to the varied configuration of the rooms, quite a number of spaces benefit from two-sided daylight exposure via corner windows.

Crosswall Construction as Hybrid Form

Chambered floor plans are essentially non-directional: there are no structural differences between the transverse and longitudinal walls. In the case of the Stone House in Tavole (1988) by Herzog & de Meuron—developed at a time when Luca Selva was a student employee at their office—this characteristic is clearly visible→32, whereby the cross-shaped reinforced-concrete structure divides the building into four spaces, which are re-traced as outlines in the elevations via the exposed reinforced-concrete frame supports. Accordingly, the longitudinal and frontal façades are basically structured in the same way. Gerhard Mack writes: "There are neither service

Die Schotten sind in Querrichtung stark aufgelöst, wirken aber durch die Tonnendächer räumlich dennoch prägend. Villa Sarabhai in Ahmedabad von Le Corbusier, 1955.

Villa Sarabhai in Ahmedabad (1955) by Le Corbusier. Although heavily dissolved transversely, because of the barrel roofs the crosswalls still exert a strong spatial effect.

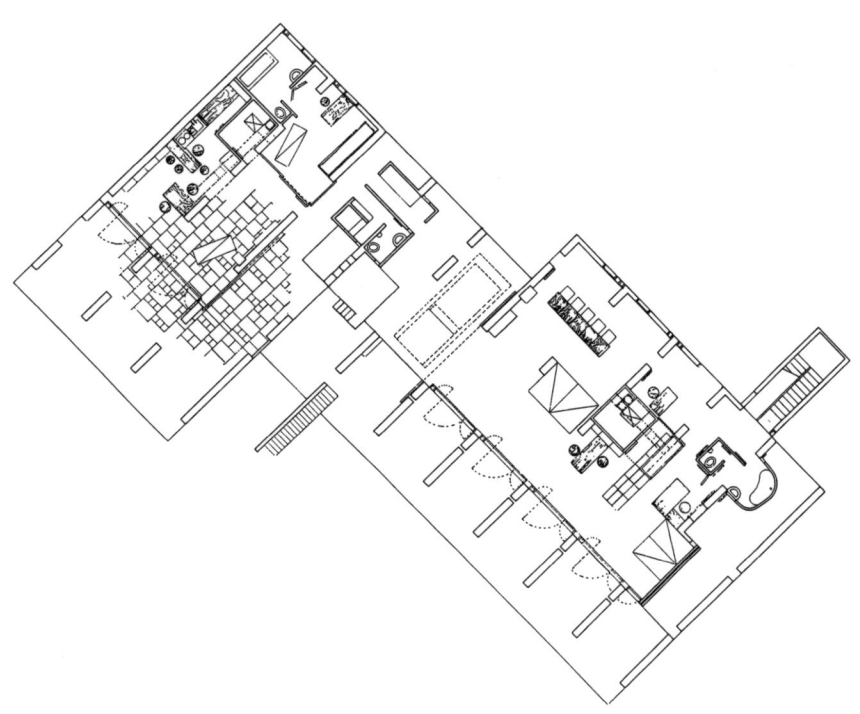

lassen sich solche Typen entsprechend unhierarchisch und frei zu kleinen und grossen Mustern entwickeln. In der Praxis weicht diese Gleichberechtigung aus ökonomisch-konstruktiven Gründen jedoch oft einer Hierarchisierung. So ist auch bei der Primarschule Erlenmatt eine klare Richtung erkennbar, die aus der Logik der Überspannung der Turnhalle abgeleitet in Querrichtung verläuft. Somit verbindet sich die Kammerung mit einer Schottenstruktur.

Le Corbusier liess in seiner berühmten Gegenüberstellung von Massiv- und Skelettbau zur Illustration der *Fünf Punkte einer Neuen Architektur* diese Mischform bewusst aus → 36, damit der Kontrast zwischen der althergebrachten Kammerung und dem offenen Grundriss möglichst gross erscheint.[20] Nichtsdestotrotz verwendete er in seinem späteren Werk die Schottenbauweise ebenfalls, etwa bei der Villa Sarabhai in Ahmedabad (1955) → 39 oder den Maisons Jaoul in Neuilly-sur-Seine (1956).

Passenderweise wählten Luca Selva und sein Team das Kennwort «Sarabhai» für den bereits erwähnten Wettbewerb in Erlenbach → 6: Auch hier ist der Kammerung eine Schottenstruktur zugrunde gelegt, die einmal längs und einmal quer verläuft. Ergänzt werden die tragenden Mauern durch im rechten Winkel dazu angeordnete, leichte Trennwände. Als weitere Referenz und generelle Inspirationsquelle für die Beschäftigung mit dem Kammergrundriss kann das würfelförmige Gebäude mit Innenhof der KNSM- und Java-Eiland-Wohnhäuser in Amsterdam von Diener & Diener (2001) genannt werden: Dieses ist aus acht Raumschichten aufgebaut, die mittels Zwischenwänden in unterschiedliche Typen eingeteilt sind → 45. Die Wohnungen selbst werden über einen Laubengang im Hof erschlossen.[21]

Noch markanter als bei der Wohnüberbauung Sandfelsen zeigt sich die Schottenstruktur bei den Wettbewerben für das Sekundarschulhaus Sandgruben in Basel (2012) → 19 und dem Gemeindezentrum Pratteln (2018). Sechs beziehungsweise acht Raumschichten sind hintereinandergelegt

hallways nor a truly habitable center. The rooms adjoin each other and create a structure as though four houses had been compressed into a conglomerate from the outside and the concrete supports were left behind as joints whose fusion process can still be seen."[19]

Because there is no particular orientation inherent in chambered floor plans, such types can be correspondingly developed non-hierarchically and freely as a range of small and large patterns. In practice, however, this equivalence often gives way to hierarchization for economic and constructive reasons. In this sense a clear alignment at the Erlenmatt Primary Schoolhouse is also recognizable, which, deriving from the logic of spanning the sports hall, runs in a crosswise direction. As a consequence, the chambering is combined with a crosswall structure.

In his famous juxtaposition of solid and skeleton-frame construction used to illustrate his "Five Points Towards a New Architecture," Le Corbusier deliberately left out this hybrid form → 36 so that the contrast between traditional chambering and the open floor plan appears as great as possible.[20] Nonetheless, he also used crosswall construction in his later work; for example, for the Villa Sarabhai in Ahmedabad (1955) → 39 or the Maisons Jaoul in Neuilly-sur-Seine (1956).

Fittingly, Luca Selva and his team chose the keyword "Sarabhai" for the aforementioned Sandfelsen housing development competition in Erlenbach → 6: Here, too, the chambering is based on a crosswall structure that runs alternately lengthways or crossways. Lightweight partition walls arranged at right angles complement the load-bearing walls. A further valuable reference and general source of inspiration for dealing with chambered floor plans is the cube-shaped building with an inner courtyard in Diener & Diener's KNSM and Java Islands residential complex in Amsterdam (2001). The development is made up of eight spatial layers, which are subdivided into different types using partition walls → 45.

und unterstreichen die Längenentwicklung der Gebäude. Im Innern halten sich bei beiden Projekten Schotten und Kammerung in etwa die Waage; beim Gemeindezentrum zeichnet sich die Schottenstruktur jedoch auch in den Stirnfassaden ab und wird damit zum prägenden Thema des Entwurfs. Demgegenüber wird beim Schulhaus Erlenmatt die Gleichwertigkeit der Längs- und Querfassaden gegen aussen, wo nötig, mittels Blindfenstern betont.

Radialer versus linearer Aufbau

Kommt zu einer Kammer eine zweite, dritte und vierte hinzu, stellt sich sofort die Frage nach dem Aufbau des Grundrisses: Werden wie beim Mittelsaal- oder Hofhaus vom Zentrum ausgehend weitere Räume addiert oder legen Nutzung, Grundstück und weitere Vorgaben eine lineare Anordnung nahe?

Ein radiales, auf alle Seiten ausgreifendes Raumgefüge entspricht auf ideale Weise der unhierarchischen Ordnung als wichtiges Merkmal eines Kammergrundrisses. Im Plan des Palazzo Antonini in Udine von Andrea Palladio (Baubeginn 1556)→50 kommt dies exemplarisch zum Ausdruck, «denn als Teile einer offenen Raumfolge sind hier alle Räume unmittelbar miteinander verbunden, sie sind strukturell gleichwertig und sind weder funktional noch durch ihre Lage irgendwie determiniert. Selbst die Toiletten sind Durchgangsräume.»[22]

Insbesondere bei Bauten mit komplexen Kammergrundrissen waren bis in die Renaissance, und darüber hinaus, radiale Muster weit verbreitet. Dabei dient ein Innenhof – oder zwei wie beim Haus der Königin in Greenwich von Inigo Jones (1635)→53 – der Belichtung, teilweise auch der Erschliessung. Beim Palazzo Strozzi in Florenz von Benedetto da Maiano (1536)→62 etwa wurde das Motiv des zentralen Peristylhofs in einen im Piano Nobile verglasten und unterteilten Umgang übertragen, von dem aus die

The apartments themselves are accessible via a loggia or exterior gallery in the courtyard.[21]

Even more striking than in the proposal for the Sandfelsen housing development are the crosswall structures in the competitions for the Sandgruben Secondary School in Basel (2012)→19 and the Pratteln Community Center (2018). Six and eight layers of space, respectively, are laid one behind the other and underscore the development of the length of the building. In the interior of both projects, crosswall and chambering strike a rough balance. In the community center, however, the crosswall structure is also evident in the shorter frontal façades so that it becomes the formative theme of the design. In contrast, in the Erlenmatt Primary Schoolhouse, the equivalence of the longitudinal and transverse façades is emphasized on the exterior, where necessary, by means of blind windows.

Radial Versus Linear Organization

If a second, third, and fourth chamber are added to an initial one, the question that immediately poses itself is how the floor plan should be organized: Are further rooms to be added from the center, as in the historical middle room or courtyard house, or do usage, plot, and other specifications suggest a linear arrangement?

A radial spatial development, extending on all sides, accords with an important ideal of the chambered floor plan, namely its non-hierarchical organization. This is exemplarily expressed in the plan of the Palazzo Antonini in Udine (begun in 1556) by Andrea Palladio→50: "For all rooms in this plan are directly linked to one another as parts of an open sequence of rooms; they are equal in terms of structural prominence and are entirely indeterminate with regard to function or placement. Even the lavatories are connecting spaces."[22] Especially in buildings with complex chambered floor plans, radial patterns

Wohnräume betreten werden.²³ Abgesehen von diesem zwar breiten, aber doch lauben- oder hallenartigen Bereich dominieren herrschaftliche Kammern, die entlang der Fassaden untereinander verbunden sind.

Ebenso verbreitet sind bei Kammergrundrissen lineare Abfolgen von Räumen. Ausgehend von einer Zelle wird eine zweite angefügt, die entweder direkt von aussen oder über die erste betreten werden kann. Dieses Prinzip findet sich spätestens seit dem Dreistreifen-Grundriss der alten Ägypter und kann noch heute in den einfachen bäuerlichen Behausungen im Alpenraum beobachtet werden, sei es in Stein wie früher im Tessin gebräuchlich oder in den Strickbauten Graubündens.

Die Durchwegung solcher Raumketten von Kammer zu Kammer führte im 15. Jahrhundert zur Entwicklung der Enfilade, beginnend mit dem Palazzo Venezia in Rom →64, der zeitweilig dem Papst diente, bis sie dann bei Schlössern üblich wurde.²⁴ Das Hintereinanderschalten von Räumen, verbunden mit breiten Türen in einer Flucht, eröffnete imposante Perspektiven, passend zu repräsentativen Wohnformen. Über die laterale Anordnung der Durchgänge konnte die Einsicht in die Räume beschränkt werden. Gleichzeitig blieb ihr gefasster Charakter erhalten, weil die Türen Öffnungen in der Wand und nicht geschosshoch waren.

Museen

Kein Wunder, übernahmen Museen diese Art von Gliederung: Dadurch konnte der Weg durch die Ausstellung gesteuert und konnten den Sälen unterschiedliche Charaktere verliehen werden, ohne dass ein Gefühl für den Gesamtzusammenhang verloren geht. Denn über die Enfilade entsteht eine starke räumliche Einheit trotz Kammerung. Ein inspirierendes Beispiel einer langen Abfolge von unterschiedlich grossen Ausstellungsflächen, die alle hintereinandergeschaltet sind, ist das Faaborg Museum →65 im dänischen Faaborg von Carl Petersen (1915).²⁵ Während

were widespread until the Renaissance and beyond. An inner courtyard—or two, as in the Queen's House in Greenwich (1635)→53 by Inigo Jones—is used for daylight exposure and in some cases also for circulation access. For example, at the Palazzo Strozzi in Florence (1539)→62, whose original design is attributed to Benedetto da Maiano, the motif of the central peristyle courtyard was transferred into a glazed and subdivided ambulatory in the piano nobile, from which the living quarters are entered.²³ Apart from this wide but still loggia- or hall-like area, the dominant feature of the Palazzo Strozzi is its stately chambers, which are connected to one another along the façades.

Linear sequences of spaces are also a widespread feature in chambered floor plans. Starting from one cell, a second is added, which can either be entered directly from the exterior or via the first cell. This principle has existed at least since the tripartite plans of the ancient Egyptians and can still be observed today in simple rural agricultural dwellings in the Alpine region, be it in stone, as was traditional earlier in the Ticino, or in the *Strickbauten* (literally: "knitted" log buildings) in Graubünden.

The passage thorough such a spatial sequence, proceeding from chamber to chamber, led to the development of the enfilade in the 15th century, beginning with the Palazzo Venezia in Rome (which served temporarily as a papal residence)→64, until this kind of progression eventually became customary in palaces.²⁴ The placement of spaces one after the other, connected with wide doors in alignment, opened up monumental perspectives befitting representative forms of dwelling. The view into the spaces could be narrowed by the lateral arrangement of the passageways. At the same time, their enclosed character was preserved because the doors were openings in the wall and did not extend floor-to-ceiling.

im vorderen Teil drei farblich und geometrisch verschieden ausgebildete Säle zunächst mittig und dann lateral miteinander verbunden sind, befindet sich im hinteren, schmaleren Bereich eine Enfilade mit kleinen Kabinetten.

Die spezielle Grundrissfigur ist der engen und langen Parzelle geschuldet. Aus funktionalen Gründen ist einer simplen Reihung natürlich wo immer möglich ein Rundgang vorzuziehen, weshalb Museen oft eine kompakte Form aufweisen[26] — womit sich das lineare mit dem radialen Prinzip verbindet.

So bei der Glyptothek in München von Leo von Klenze (1830) → 73, ein nahezu quadratischer Gebäudekörper mit grossem Innenhof, um den ein Kranz von je unterschiedlich proportionierten Sälen angeordnet ist. Die Belichtung erfolgt mehrheitlich über Oberlichter. Diese Art der Tageslichtversorgung ist ein wesentlicher Grund, weshalb sich Kammergrundrisse für Ausstellungsräume bestens eignen: Weil das Licht über die Decke eingebracht wird, kann eine beliebige Anzahl von Raumschichten aneinandergelegt werden, ohne dass ein Problem mit der Helligkeit entsteht.

Eines der überzeugendsten jüngeren Museen dieser Art ist der Salisbury-Flügel der Londoner National Gallery von Robert Venturi und Denise Scott Brown (1991) → 74. Vom mehrfach erweiterten Altbau setzt sich der Annex mittels rotundenartigem Verbindungsgang ab und ist als dreischichtiger Kammergrundriss organisiert. Über die höchst durchdachte Platzierung der Durchgänge — seien sie mittig, seitlich, in einer Achse oder zueinander verschoben angeordnet — sowie deren architektonische Ausbildung mit Rundbögen, rechteckigen Rahmen, Säulen oder Gebälk entstehen vielfältige Bezüge und Hierarchien zwischen den Sälen. Und noch etwas zeigt dieses Gebäude, das für die Projekte mit Kammergrundriss von Luca Selva Architekten ebenfalls gilt: Auch wenn die Ordnung streng rechtwinklig ist, kommt der Diagonale im Erleben der Räume und Raumzusammenhänge eine entscheidende Bedeutung zu.

Museums

It is no wonder that museums adopted this type of articulation: directing the route through the exhibition and giving the halls different characters without a sense of the overall context being lost was possible because despite the chambering the enfilade creates a strong spatial unity. An inspiring example of a long sequence of exhibition spaces of different sizes, all connected successively one after the other, is the Danish Faaborg Museum (1915) → 65 by Carl Petersen.[25] While the front part contains three halls—differentiated by various colors and geometries—that are initially connected in the middle and then laterally, in the rear, narrower area is an enfilade with small cabinets. The special floor plan is determined by the narrow and long parcel of land. Naturally, for functional reasons, wherever possible a simple sequence is preferable to a circular corridor, which is why museums often possess a compact form,[26] a solution that connects the linear with the radial principle.

An exemplary application of this concept is the Glyptothek in Munich (1830) → 73 by Leo von Klenze—an almost square building volume comprising a large inner courtyard with differently proportioned halls wrapped around it. Daylight exposure is provided mostly via skylights. This type of lighting is a major reason why chambered floor plans are ideally suited for exhibition rooms: because the light is brought in via the ceiling, any number of spatial layers can be juxtaposed without creating a problem with the brightness.

One of the most compelling recent museums of this kind is the Sainsbury Wing (1991) of the National Gallery in London by Robert Venturi and Denise Scott Brown → 74. The annex diverges from the old building, which has been expanded several times, by means of a rotunda-like connecting passageway and is organized as a three-layer chambered floor plan. The extremely well-thought-out placement of the passageways—be it centrally, laterally,

Wohnungsbau

Für das Zusammenspiel über die Diagonale bedarf es nicht vieler Kammern. Diese Erfahrung ist bereits in kleineren Strukturen möglich. Gerade im Wohnungsbau wirken damit die Perspektiven eindrucksvoller und die Grundrisse grösser, als sie tatsächlich sind. Zudem tragen gezielte visuelle Verbindungen zwischen den Zimmern dazu bei, dass die Kammerung nicht als beengend oder rigid wahrgenommen wird.

Kammergrundrisse sind im Wohnungsbau von alters her am meisten verbreitet. Ambivalent dazu verhielten sich jedoch die Architekten der Moderne: Einerseits propagierten viele in Abkehr von der Tradition den fliessenden, offenen Grundriss, andererseits wurde auf der Suche nach der Wohnung für das Existenzminimum der flächensparende Charakter des Kammergrundrisses als Vorteil erkannt. Indem die Durchgangszonen den Räumen zugeschlagen wurden, konnte die Quadratmeterzahl niedrig gehalten und trotzdem eine gewisse Grosszügigkeit der Wohnung erreicht werden.

Genau diese Strategie schlugen die Autoren des Buches *Sozialer Wohnungs- und Siedlungsbau* in der Schweiz während des Zweiten Weltkrieges vor: «Nach reiflicher Abwägung aller Vor- und Nachteile wird vorgeschlagen, die Küche nur als Kochküche auszubilden, sie jedoch unmittelbar an den Wohnraum anzuschliessen und die Schlafzimmer von diesem her zugänglich zu machen. Man erspart damit den Korridor, seine Bodenfläche wird zum Wohnraum geschlagen, dieser wird von der Küche her geheizt, auch die Schlafzimmer werden durch den gleichen Ofen vom Wohnraum aus temperiert.»[27] →80

Die minutiös vermassten Typengrundrisse, die als Anregung für die Praxis zu verstehen waren, sind von Interesse, weil sie ein weiteres Prinzip zur erfolgreichen Strukturierung von Kammergrundrissen darstellen, das Luca Selva Architekten ebenfalls anwenden: die Verschiebung der Kammern zueinander, wodurch sich die Verbindung in an axis, or offset from one another— and their architectural definition through round or semicircular arches, rectangular frames, columns, or entablatures, create a variety of references and hierarchies between the halls. Moreover, this building evinces a further feature, which also applies to the projects with a chambered floor plan by Luca Selva Architekten: even when the plan organization is stringently rectangular, the diagonal plays a decisively important role in the lived experience of the spaces and the spatial coherence.

Residential Buildings

Creating a spatial interplay along the diagonal does not require many chambers; indeed, this experience is already possible in smaller structures. Particularly in residential buildings, the effects of the perspectives are more impressive and the floor plans seem larger than they actually are. In addition, deliberately conceived visual connections between rooms help ensure that the chambering is not perceived as too confining or rigid.

From time immemorial, chambered floor plans have been most widespread in residential buildings. In this sense, however, the approach of Modernist architects was ambiguous: on the one hand, turning away from tradition, many propagated the flowing, open floor plan; on the other hand, in searching to create a minimum subsistence dwelling, the space-saving character of the chambered floor plan was recognized as an advantage. By incorporating the passageway zones into the rooms, the number of square meters could be kept low while still achieving a certain generosity in the apartment.

Precisely this strategy is proposed by the contributors to the publication *Sozialer Wohnungs- und Siedlungsbau* (Building social housing and settlements) for Switzerland during World War II: "After carefully weighing all the advantages and disadvantages, it is recommended to design the kitchen only for cooking and food preparation,

Schottenbauweise oder Kammergrundriss? Die regelmässigen Abstände der Längs- und die freie Anordnung der Querwände erzeugen diese Ambivalenz. Sie ist aber nur plangrafischer Art, räumlich wirksam ist das Kammerprinzip. Wohnhaus in Amsterdam von Diener & Diener, 2001.

Courtyard building, KNSM and Java Islands residential project (2001), Amsterdam, by Diener & Diener. Crosswall construction or chambered floor plan? The regular spacing of the longitudinal and the open arrangement of the transverse walls produce this ambiguity. However, this seeming polarity is simply graphic, based on the plans: the real spatial effect is generated by the chambering principle.

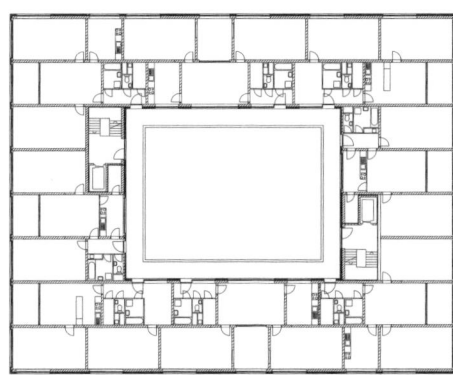

← Plan 23

der Räume einfacher gestaltet. Bei den kleineren, nordostseitig gelegenen Wohnungen des Mehrfamilienhauses in Aarburg (2017) →57 beispielsweise lässt sich dies gut nachvollziehen: Deren Grundriss ist so aufgebaut, dass beim Weg durch die Wohnung eine schlangenförmige Bewegung entsteht, die wechselweise von der einen zur anderen Raumschicht führt, weil die Querwände zueinander verschoben und die Türen an den Längsseiten platziert sind. Damit öffnen sich immer wieder neue Perspektiven und Ausblicke.

In abgeschwächter Form findet sich dieses Motiv auch bei den grossen Wohnungen, die durchgängig organisiert sind und damit alle vier Raumschichten benutzen. Zentrales Element ist hier jedoch die Loggia: Über den eingezogenen Aussenraum wird Tageslicht in die Tiefe des Gebäudes gelenkt und damit der Wohnraum im hinteren Bereich mit verblüffend viel Tageslicht versorgt. Es entsteht ein ganz eigener räumlicher Schwerpunkt, der die Atmosphäre der Wohnung prägt.

Beim bereits erwähnten Projekt in Köln ergänzen Wohnbauten mit vier bis sechs Raumschichten das bestehende vormalige Industrieensemble →58. Die Basler Architekten vereinigen die verschiedensten Formen von Kammergrundrissen und loten das gesamte Spektrum an Möglichkeiten aus. Auch hier werden über Loggien, die Verschiebung der Kammern zueinander, unterschiedlich breite Verbindungen zwischen den Räumen, teilweise gestaffelte Baukörper und die geschickte Dimensionierung der Raumschichten und Kammern abwechslungsreiche, speziell geschnittene Wohnungen entworfen.

Kammergrundriss in der dritten Dimension

Noch komplexer werden Kammergrundrisse bei einer Erweiterung in die dritte Dimension. Auch damit haben Luca Selva Architekten bereits mehrfach experimentiert. «Tetris» hiess passenderweise das Motto beim

yet directly connect it to the living area, from where the bedrooms are also made accessible. Thereby the usual space for the corridor can be spared and rather added onto the living room, which is heated from the kitchen, and, as well, the same stove can warm the bedrooms with heat conveyed from the living room."[27] →80

These meticulously dimensioned floor plan types, which were meant to be understood as an impulse for architectural praxis, are of interest because they represent another principle in the successful structuring of chambered floor plans that Luca Selva Architekten also employ: the displacement or shifting of the chambers relative to each other, making it easier to create a connection between the spaces. This is easily identifiable, for example, in the smaller northeast facing apartments in the multi-family residential building in Aarburg (2017) →57: their floor plan is laid out in such a way that in moving through the apartment, a snake-like path emerges, which alternately leads from one spatial layer to another. This is because the transverse walls are staggered in relation to each other and the doors are positioned at the longitudinal sides, an arrangement that allows new perspectives and external views to be frequently opened up.

This motif can also be found in a softened form in the large apartments, which are organized uniformly using all four spatial layers. The main feature here, however, is the loggia: daylight is channeled into the depths of the building via the recessed outdoor space, which provides the living space at the rear with an astonishing amount of daylight. The result is a very special spatial accent that distinguishes the atmosphere of the apartments.

In the aforementioned project in Cologne, residential buildings with four to six spatial layers complement the existing industrial ensemble →58. The Basel architects combine the most diverse forms of chambered floor plans and explore the entire spectrum of possibilities. Here, too, diverse, specially

Projektwettbewerb für das Gemeindezentrum in Pratteln: Die gekammerte Schottenstruktur wurde im Schnitt mittels doppelgeschossiger Lounge- und Info-/Servicezone der Bibliothek sowie drei eingeschnittenen, unterschiedlich grossen Höfen unter Spannung gesetzt.

Im Wohnungsbau denkt man bei dreidimensionalen Zellenstrukturen natürlich sofort an den Raumplan von Adolf Loos, der bei seinen Villen innerhalb einfacher Kubaturen höchst kontrastreiche Raumfiguren schuf. Ein Grossteil ihrer Wirkung beruht — beispielsweise bei der Villa Müller in Prag (1930) — auf den unterschiedlichen Höhen und Proportionen der Haupträume sowie deren Zusammenspiel, das über Treppen, Durchblicke, Verbindungselemente und die Materialisierung orchestriert wird. Obwohl dem Prinzip nach ein Kammergrundriss, bilden die Repräsentationsräume samt Treppenhaus einen gegliederten, aber offen zusammenhängenden Organismus → 88.

Aus demselben Jahr wie die Villa Müller stammt das Eigenheim von Lux Guyer, das Einfamilienhaus Sunnebüel in Küsnacht-Itschnach (1930) → 94. Auch hier kommt ein Kammergrundriss zur Anwendung, der über die zweigeschossige Treppenhalle eine starke Verbindung zwischen den Hauptgeschossen herstellt. Teilweise können die Kammern, wie bei Projekten dieser Architektin üblich, mittels Schiebe- und Klapptüren in unterschiedlichem Grad geöffnet werden. Dadurch entstehen überraschende Raumzusammenhänge in der Horizontalen, die an eine Enfilade oder Innenräume japanischer Holzhäuser mit ihren leichten Schiebeelementen denken lassen. Der Vergleich kommt nicht von ungefähr, wurde doch ein patentiertes Holzbausystem verwendet, das dem Grundriss eine modulare Ordnung zugrunde legt.[28]

Diese Konstruktionsweise verleiht dem Haus einen durchgehenden Rhythmus, der sich im Äusseren über die Positionierung und Teilung der Fenster ebenfalls zeigt. Anders bei den Bauten von Loos: Die Öffnungen mit ihren unterschiedlichen Formaten scheinen

designed apartment layouts are created via loggias, shifting chambers vis-à-vis each other, varied-width connections between spaces, partially staggered building volumes, and sophisticated dimensioning of the spatial layers and chambers.

Chambered Floor Plans
in the Third Dimension

Chambered floor plans become even more complex when extended into the third dimension. Luca Selva Architekten have also already experimented with this aspect several times. The fitting motto "Tetris" was coined for the Pratteln Community Center competition entry, where spatial tension was created by integrating a double-story lounge area, a library information/service zone, and three incised courtyards of different sizes within the chambered crosswall structure.

When considering three-dimensional cellular structures in residential buildings, what immediately comes to mind is Adolf Loos's approach to spatial planning for his villas in which he created richly contrasting spatial figures within simple cubic volumes. A large part of the effect is based—for example, in the Villa Müller in Prague (1930)—on the different heights and proportions of the main spaces as well as their interplay, which is orchestrated via stairs, views, connecting elements, and the materials of construction. Although the principle is based on a chambered floor plan, the representative spaces, including the staircase, form an articulated but openly cohesive organism → 88.

Lux Guyer's own home, the Sunnebüel (1930) → 94, a single-family dwelling in Küsnacht-Itschnach, dates from the same year as the Villa Müller. Here, too, a chambered floor plan is applied, which creates a strong connection between the main floors via a double-story stairway hall. Typical for the architect's projects, some of the chambers can be opened up to different degrees via sliding and folding doors. This creates surprising spatial interrelationships horizontally,

beinahe zufällig gesetzt, verbergen eher, was sich im Innern abspielt, als dass sie die Raumeinteilung preisgeben würden. Ähnlich verhält es sich beim Generationenhaus in Binningen von Luca Selva Architekten (2013) → 105: Die höchst komplexe Verschränkung von zwei Wohnungen ist dem Gebäude von aussen nicht anzusehen. Allein die Setzung der Fenster lässt teils höhere Räume vermuten. Im Innern spielen die Architekten alle Trümpfe eines dreidimensionalen Kammergrundrisses aus. Allein schon die Wege durch das Haus, die völlig unterschiedlich verlaufen, sind voller Überraschungen. Das hat sehr viel damit zu tun, dass die Treppenhäuser nicht durchgehend sind. Dank dieser Massnahme sowie der räumlichen Verschachtelung sind beide Wohnungen allseitig orientiert und profitieren damit gleichermassen vom Park und der Aussicht auf die Stadt Basel. Zudem erzeugen einzelne überhohe Räume einen vertikalen Sog, die dem Kammergrundriss eine unerwartete Dynamik verleihen.

Vom Einzelgebäude zum Städtebau

Ob vertikal oder auf einer Ebene, ob radial oder linear organisiert, Kammergrundrisse führen nicht zwangsläufig zu einem kompakten Gebäudekörper. Von römischen Villen über mittelalterliche Klosteranlagen bis zu englischen Landhäusern des 19. Jahrhunderts präsentieren sich Bauten mit Kammergrundrissen bisweilen als raumgreifende, vielgestaltige Konglomerate.

Das gilt auch für den Beitrag zur Zentrumsüberbauung Areal Hübeli in Aesch (2010) von Luca Selva Architekten → 8, wo sie dieses Ordnungsprinzip in einen städtebaulichen Massstab übersetzten: Sieben Häuser mit Satteldach sind so aneinandergeschoben, dass eine zusammenhängende Struktur aus gekammerten Wohnungsgrundrissen entsteht. Sie schliesst die Baulücke entlang der Strasse und lotet von dort ausgehend die ganze Tiefe der Parzelle aus. Über Versätze der Gebäudekörper

recalling an enfilade or the interiors of Japanese wooden houses with their lightweight sliding elements. The comparison is no coincidence, as a patented system using prefabricated wood elements was used which bases the floor plan on a modular scheme.[28]

This means of construction lends the house a continuous rhythm, which is also reflected in the exterior through the positioning and division of the windows. In Loos's buildings, the approach is different: the openings with their varying formats seem to be positioned almost at random, tending to conceal what is going on inside rather than revealing the spatial layout. The same is true of the Haus am Park project in Binningen (2013) → 105, a multi-generational house by Luca Selva Architekten, where the extremely complex interlacing of two apartments is invisible on the exterior of the building. Only the placement of the windows suggests that the interior spaces might be greater in height. In the interior, the architects exploit the stratagem of a three-dimensional chambered floor plan to its full extent. Considered solely by themselves, the routes through the house, which proceed in completely different ways, are full of surprises. This stems largely from the fact that the staircases are not continuous. On account of these measures and the spatial intertwinement, both apartments are oriented in all directions, benefitting equally from the park and the view of the city of Basel. In addition, individual extra-high spaces exert a vertical pull, lending the chambered floor plan an unexpected dynamism.

From Single Buildings to Urban Planning

Whether organized vertically or on one level, whether radially or linearly, chambered floor plans do not necessarily lead to a compact building volume. Indeed, considering a range of typologies, from Roman villas to medieval monastery complexes and beyond to 19th-century English country houses, there are occasional examples of

Die unhierarchische Gliederung eines Kammergrundrisses kommt beim Palazzo Antonini in Udine gut zum Ausdruck. Selbst die Toiletten sind als Durchgangsräume konzipiert und ordnen sich in die Raumfolge ein. Andrea Palladio, ab 1556.

Exemplary non-hierarchical division of the chambered floor plan in the Palazzo Antonini (1556), Udine, by Andrea Palladio. Even the lavatories are conceived as connecting spaces and are subsumed within the overall sequence of rooms.

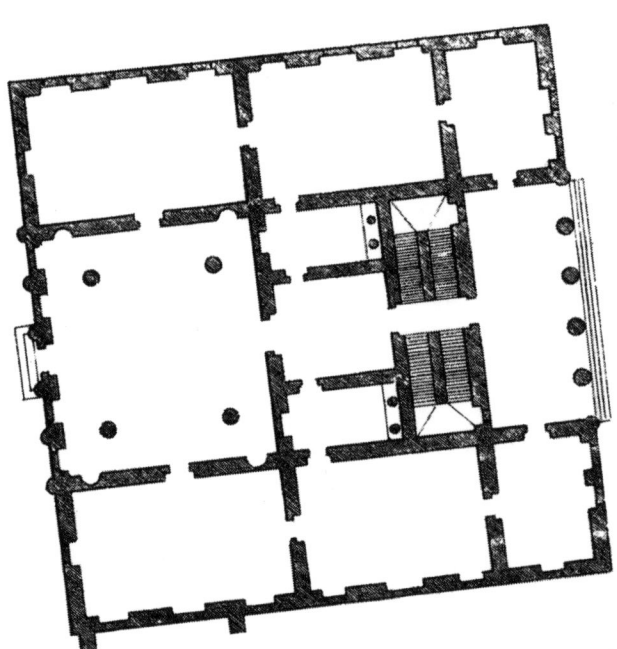

entstehen teils hofartige, teils offenere Aussenräume. Der Wechsel von der strassenbegleitenden Ausrichtung der durchlaufenden Zwischenwände hin zur Betonung der Parzellentiefe erfolgt auf selbstverständliche Weise und übersetzt das Muster einer typisch ländlichen Bauweise — Wohnhaus an der Strasse, Ökonomiegebäude im rückwärtigen Teil — in die Morphologie der Gesamtstruktur.

Wie dieses Beispiel zeigt, beschränkt sich das System des Kammergrundrisses nicht auf die Anwendung bei einem einzelnen Gebäude. Das additive Prinzip ermöglicht eine beliebige Ausdehnung und eignet sich deshalb bestens für die städtebauliche Dimension. Davon zeugt bereits der Siedlungsplan von Çatal Höyük, der, wie eingangs beschrieben, nichts anderes ist als eine Ansammlung von Häusern in Form einzelner Zellen, die Mauer an Mauer gebaut sind. Strassen und Gassen fehlen, weil die Häuser über das Dach betreten wurden.

Dieses komplett unhierarchische Muster stösst schnell an seine Grenzen, weshalb in der Folge urbane Siedlungen oft mittels übergeordneter Elemente wie öffentlicher Bauten, Strassen und Freiräume gegliedert wurden. Allein, bei den für den Orient seit Urzeiten typischen Hofhaussiedlungen wurde die Stadt weiterhin — anders als in der westlichen Welt — vom Haus aus gedacht: Strassen, Plätze und Gassen wurden als Resträume aufgefasst, die nicht oder noch nicht überbaut sind; Umfassungsmauer und Parzellengrenze sind identisch.[29] Durch innere Verdichtung wurden im Lauf der Generationen die Lücken zwischen den Häusern schrittweise geschlossen und die Höfe aufgrund zusätzlich benötigter Räume immer kleiner. Als Folge davon nahm die Gliederung der Gebäude an Komplexität zu. Sie entwickelten sich teils über mehrere Geschosse, und der Verlauf der Gassen passte sich immer wieder an die neue Situation an.[30] Neben der Parzellenstruktur, die kaum angetastet wurde,[31] bildet somit das Prinzip der Höfe, von denen aus die einzelnen Kammern direkt betreten werden, die einzige Konstante.

buildings with chambered floor plans which are spread-out, multifaceted conglomerates.

The same applies to the proposal for the Hübeli Works Site Development in Aesch (2010) by Luca Selva Architekten→8, in which they take this principle of organization and translate it to the scale of urban planning: seven residential buildings with gable roofs are pushed together in such a way that a cohesive structure of chambered apartment floor plans is created. This closes the gap in the street line and, starting from there, is developed to extend the entire depth of the plot. Offsetting the building volumes creates partly courtyard-like and partly more open outdoor spaces. The change from the street-side alignment of the continuous partition walls to emphasizing the depth of the lot takes place naturally and translates a typical rural construction pattern—dwelling at the street, sheds and barn to the rear—into the morphology of the overall structure.

As this example shows, application of the chambered floor plan system is not limited to a single building. The additive principle can be expanded at will and is therefore ideally suited for an urban-planning scale. This is already evident in the plan of the Çatalhöyük settlement, which, as described earlier, is nothing more than a collection of houses in the form of individual cells that are built wall-to-wall. There were no streets or alleys because the houses were entered through the roof.

Nevertheless, this completely nonhierarchical pattern quickly reaches its natural limits, which is why urban settlements are often structured using superordinate elements such as public buildings, streets, and open spaces. Solely in terms of the courtyard-house settlements typical of the ancient Near East—and as opposed to in later Western civilizations—the city was still conceived as starting from the house: streets, squares, and alleys were considered as residual spaces that had nothing built on them—or, at least, not yet; enclosing walls and lot boundaries are

So gleicht etwa der historische Stadtgrundriss von Aleppo in Syrien →98, das seit 3000 v. Chr. ununterbrochen besiedelt ist, einem Palimpsest, bestehend aus einer unübersehbaren, sich laufend verändernden Anzahl und Gestalt an Hofhäusern, gebaut aus Kalkstein. Ein solcher Gebäudeteppich kennzeichnet etwa Banqusa, ein östlich an die Altstadt grenzendes Wohnquartier, dessen Bausubstanz ins 18. Jahrhundert zurückreicht.[32] Typische Hausgrundrisse zeigen eine verschlungene Raumstruktur, die sich im Lauf der Zeit verändert hat: Wie bei einem Puzzle →100 greifen die einzelnen Kammern und Höfe ineinander, als Abbild der Familien- und Besitzergeschichte.[33]

Auch im ländlichen Raum gibt es Dörfer, die aus einer Ansammlung von Häusern mit gekammerten Grundrissen bestehen. Ein gut dokumentiertes Beispiel mit einem hohen Anteil an Kammergrundrissen ist Soglio im Bergell →102. Unter anderem an diesem Ort führte Michael Alder mit Studierenden der heutigen FHNW in Muttenz in den 1970er- bis 1990er-Jahren typologische Studien durch. Das Resultat sind aufwendig gezeichnete Grundriss-, Schnitt- und Ansichtspläne, die das Einzelgebäude im Kontext von Siedlung und Landschaft zeigen.[34]

Holz- und Steinhäuser ergänzen sich. Vorherrschend sind Einzelbauten mit schmalen Durchgängen dazwischen, und «wo kein Weg hindurchführt, rücken die Bauten noch näher zusammen oder bilden bauliche Komplexe».[35] Gärten oder private Aussenräume finden sich keine im Dorf, sie wurden an die Peripherie verdrängt.[36] Anders als in Aleppo sind hier aber die Hauptgassen sowie der Platz die bestimmenden Elemente, denen sich die Häuser unterordnen. Faszinierend ist die morphologische Struktur auch deshalb, weil – abgesehen von der Kirche und den palastartigen Bürgerhäusern der Salis als bestimmendem Geschlecht in Soglio – alle Bauten, ob Stall, Scheune oder Wohnhaus, ähnliche Dimensionen aufweisen. Diese beruhen auf einer identical.[29] Through internal densification over generations, the gaps between houses were gradually closed and the courtyards became smaller and smaller owing to the additional spaces that were required. As a result, the spatial subdivision of the buildings increased in complexity. In part they were developed over several floors, and the course of the alleys was continuously adapted to the new situation.[30] Consequently, the only constant feature—besides the plot structure, which was hardly ever altered[31]—was the principle of the courtyards, from which the individual chambers were entered directly.

In this sense the historical urban layout of Aleppo in Syria →98, which has been continuously inhabited since 3000 BC, is like a palimpsest, where an unmistakable, constantly changing number and shape of courtyard houses built of limestone are overlaid. This carpet of buildings is characteristic, for instance, of Banqusa, a residential quarter bordering the historic center to the east, which dates back to the 18th century.[32] Typical house floor plans show a labyrinthine spatial structure that has changed over time: like a puzzle →100, the individual courtyards and chambers interlock, reflecting the history of the families and owners.[33]

In rural areas, too, there are villages that consist of a collection of houses with chambered floor plans. A well-documented example with a high quota of chambered floor plans is Soglio in Bergell →102. Here, among other places, Michael Alder carried out typological studies with students at what is now the University of Applied Sciences and Arts Northwestern Switzerland (FHNW) in Muttenz from the 1970s to the 1990s. The results are recorded in elaborately drawn floor plans, sections, and elevations that show the individual building in the context of the settlement and the landscape.[34]

Wooden and stone houses complement each other. Individual buildings with narrow passageways in between predominate, and "where there is no path leading through, the buildings

Vom antiken Hofhaus bis zu den Palästen der Renaissance und darüber hinaus war der radiale Aufbau von Kammergrundrissen weit verbreitet. Beim Haus der Königin in Greenwich (1635) von Inigo Jones wird der zentrale Raum über zwei Höfe belichtet.

Queen's House (1635), Greenwich, by Inigo Jones, with daylight for the central room provided by two courtyards. From the courtyard house of antiquity to the palaces of the Renaissance and beyond, the radial development of chambered floor plans is widespread.

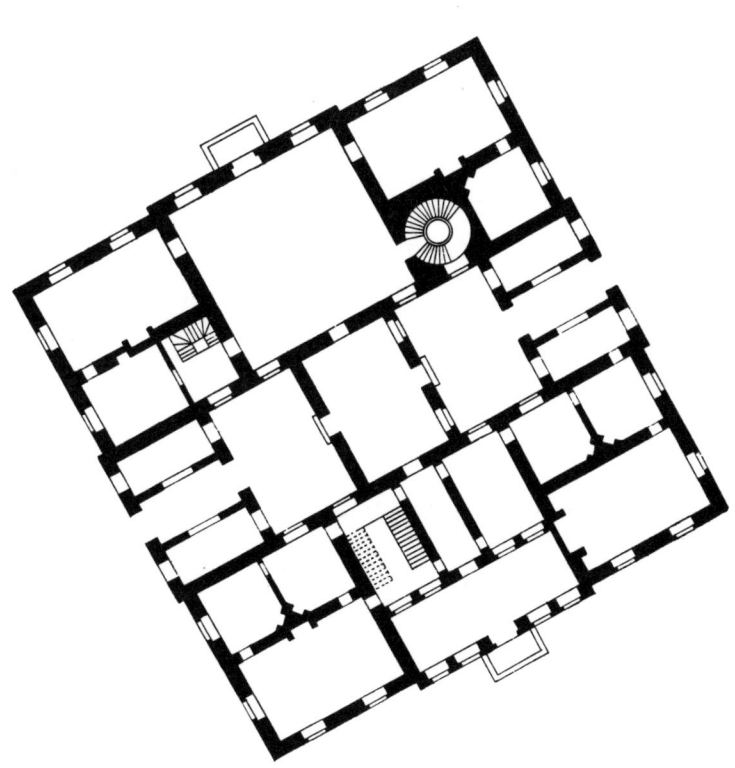

konstruktiven Ökonomie der Mittel, die ja den Ursprung der Kammerbauweise bildet.

Handschrift und Ausdrucksform

Wie Annette Spiro in ihrem Buch zum Bauplan schreibt, ist dieser «ein technisches Werkzeug: sachlich, verbindlich, genau. Er verschleiert und beschönigt nicht, er will nicht interpretiert, sondern eindeutig gelesen werden. Seine Zeichensprache muss sich an Normen und Konventionen halten. Und trotzdem – oder gerade deshalb? – ist er ein einzigartiges Ausdrucksmittel und trägt die Handschrift des Architekten.»[37] Das zeigen auch die Pläne von Luca Selva Architekten, die sich dem Kammergrundriss widmen.

Natürlich hat sich in den Jahren, seit sich das Büro mit diesem Typ auseinandersetzt, die Plangrafik ebenso verändert, wie der Wissensstand gewachsen ist. Allen, auch den ersten Grundrissen, ist jedoch das tiefe Interesse an und die forschende Auseinandersetzung mit dem Thema der Kammerung anzusehen. Mittlerweile besticht vor allem die Kompaktheit und Vielfalt der gefundenen Lösungen, die gleichwohl selbstverständlich und grosszügig anmuten.

Erstaunlich ist, wie unterschiedlich sich Kammergrundrisse bilden lassen. Davon zeugen nicht zuletzt die im Text erwähnten historischen Beispiele. Obwohl zellenartige Raumstrukturen für die verschiedensten Bauaufgaben geeignet sind, müssen sie sich trotzdem jedes Mal neu beweisen. Denn die strenge Ordnung der Kammerung wirkt auf dem Papier einschränkender als in der Realität, was in der Planungsphase den Bauträgern vermittelt werden muss.

Ihrer Wandel- und Erweiterbarkeit wegen sind Kammergrundrisse ein gutes Mittel, um den heutigen Anforderungen gerecht zu werden. Die Veränderung der Gesellschaft, zu der eine Abflachung der Hierarchien in den verschiedensten Bereichen gehört, hat natürlich Auswirkungen

move even closer together or form structural complexes."[35] There are no gardens or private outdoor spaces in the village; they have been pushed to the periphery.[36] Unlike in Aleppo, however, the main narrow streets and village square are the determining elements to which the houses are subordinate. The morphological structure is also fascinating because—apart from the church and the palace-like grand domiciles of the Salis, the dominant family lineage in Soglio—all buildings, whether stable, barn, or dwelling, exhibit similar dimensions. These are based on a constructive economy of means, which indeed is the origin of the chambered construction method.

Signature and Expressive Form

As Annette Spiro writes in her book on working drawings, they are: "a technical tool: factual, binding, and precise. It does not veil or embellish anything; it is not meant to be interpreted, but instead, clearly read. The symbolic language it uses must hold to norms and conventions. And nonetheless -or perhaps for that very reason? - it is an unrivaled means of expression bearing the architect's handwriting."[37] This is also evident in the plans by Luca Selva Architekten that involve chambered layouts.

Of course, in the years since the office has been working with this type the representational graphic techniques in plans have changed as the level of knowledge has grown. However, all of them, including their initial floor plans, demonstrate their deep interest in and their research-based investigations into the subject of chambering. In the meantime, what is most compelling is the compactness and diversity of the solutions that have been found, which at the same time also seem spacious and logical.

It is amazing how differently chambered floor plans can be articulated, a fact shown not only by the historical examples mentioned in this text. Although cell-like spatial structures are

auf die Architektur: Zunehmend gefragt sind Bauten, deren Räume sich den jeweiligen Bedürfnissen entsprechend anpassen und zuordnen lassen. Es mag paradox erscheinen, aber dazu eignen sich Gebäude mit «starken», determinierten Strukturen sehr gut. Am Beispiel der Wohnbauten der Gründerzeit lässt sich dies nachvollziehen: Sie sind dank gut proportionierten, gleichartigen und relativ hohen Räumen, die für die unterschiedlichsten Zwecke offen sind, bis heute beliebt. Ähnliches gilt für alle Arten von Kammergrundrissen. Weil sie im Vergleich zu anderen Typologien relativ wenig festlegen, lassen sie sich einfach den individuellen Vorstellungen entsprechend nutzen. Das Unhierarchische in Verbindung mit einer klaren, einfachen Struktur erweist sich als äusserst anpassungsfähiges Prinzip, ohne dass bauliche Massnahmen notwendig wären.

Luca Selva Architekten haben im Lauf der Jahre ein eigenes Vokabular des Kammergrundrisses entwickelt, eine eigene Logik, wie sie die Räume, Nutzungen, Öffnungen, Ein- und Durchblicke miteinander in Beziehung setzen können. Übergeordnetes Ziel bleibt dabei der Wunsch, den Gebäuden eine Beständigkeit und Gebrauchstauglichkeit zu verleihen, die dem Wesen dieser fundamentalen Entwurfsweise gerecht wird und ihr immer wieder ein neues, unerwartetes Kapitel hinzufügt.

suitable for the most varied of building tasks, they still have to be justified anew every time, especially since the strict arrangement of chambering has a more restrictive effect on paper than in reality, which needs to be conveyed to the building client in the planning phase.

Because of their capacity to be transformed and expanded, chambered floor plans are a good means of meeting contemporary requirements. Needless to say, social changes, which include the flattening of hierarchies in numerous different spheres, have also had an impact on architecture: there is increasing demand for buildings whose spaces can be adapted and matched to the respective occupant's needs. It may seem paradoxical, but buildings with "strong," determinate structures prove very suitable in this respect. This is clearly illustrated by residential buildings from the German Gründerzeit era, which are still popular today on account of their well-proportioned, homogeneous, and relatively high-ceilinged spaces that can freely accommodate a wide variety of purposes. The same applies to all kinds of chambered floor plans. Because they pre-determine relatively little in comparison to other typologies, they can easily be used according to individual preferences. The non-hierarchical in connection with a clear, simple structure proves to be an extremely adaptable principle, without the need for extraneous constructive measures.

Over the years, Luca Selva Architekten have developed their own vocabulary for the chambered floor plan—a particular logic of how spaces, usages, openings, and interior and exterior perspectives can be combined in relationship with each other. In doing so, the overriding aim remains the desire to lend the buildings a durability and fitness for use that does justice to the essence of this fundamental method and process of design, continuing each time to add a new and unexpected chapter.

Im Mittelpunkt dieses städtebaulichen Projekts stand eine Quartierentwicklung nach den Vorgaben der 2000-Watt-Gesellschaft. Die beiden als Vierspänner organisierten und mit je zwei Liften und Treppenhäusern im Innern erschlossenen Wohnbauten liefern gültige Antworten auf Fragen zum Kammergrundriss; ausgeführt wurden sie im Holzbau. Gebietsentwicklung «Gishalde – Steinbille», Oberstadt Aarburg, Studienauftrag auf Einladung, Artemis Immobilien AG: 2014; Fertigstellung: 2017.

The focus of this urban development project was the development of a neighborhood to meet the specifications of the 2000-Watt Society. Executed in wood, the two residential buildings are laid out with four separate units per floor, accessible internally via two elevators and two staircases. This project provides convincing answers to questions about the chambered floor plan. Gishalde-Steinbille development district, Oberstadt, Aarburg, invited study commission, Artemis Immobilien AG: 2014; completion: 2017.

← ↓

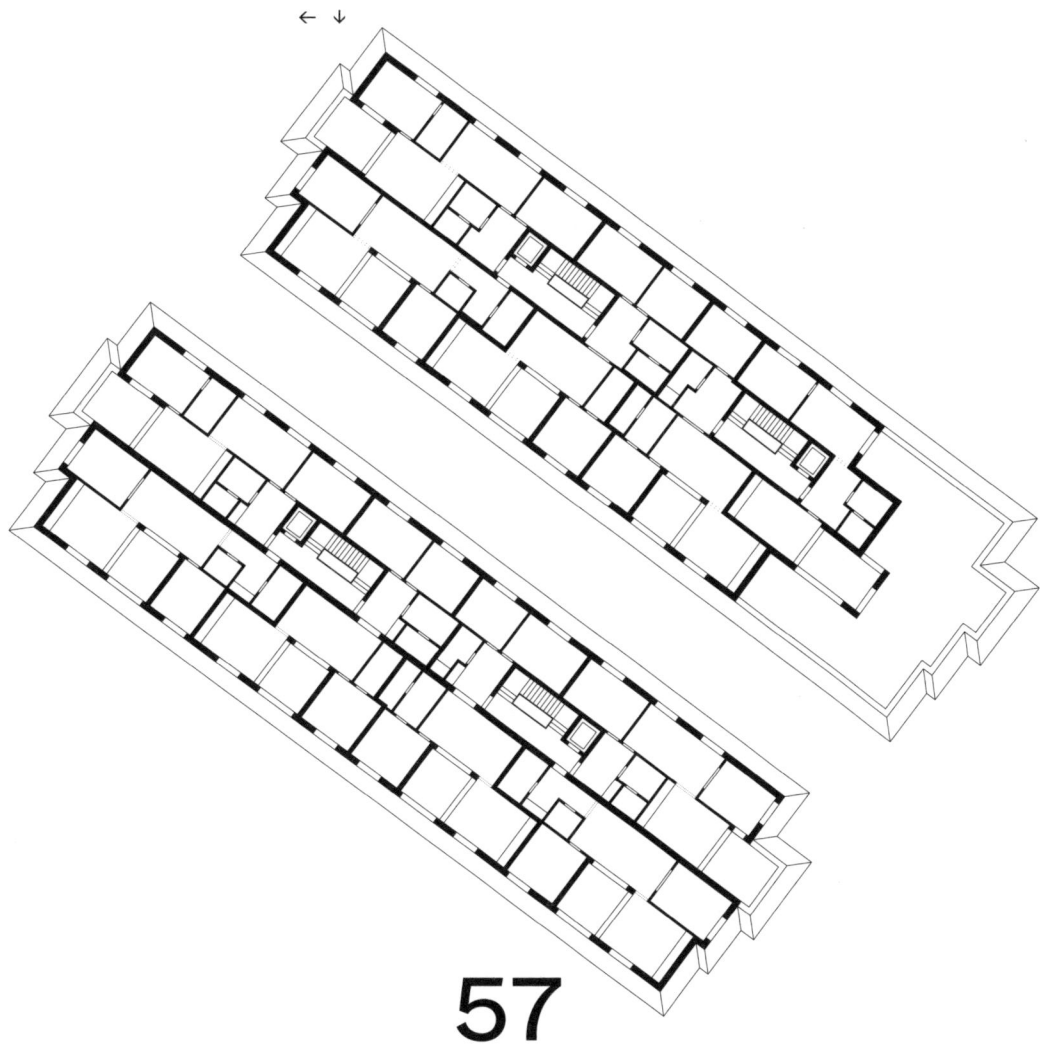

Ein bestehendes ehemaliges Industrieareal soll weitergebaut werden. Aufbauend auf einem städtebaulichen Plan von Luca Selva Architekten verbinden sich die Neubauten in ihren Volumen und strukturell mit den denkmalgeschützten Gebäuden der früheren Baumwollbleiche. Als Replik auf die Hallenbauten des Bestands werden bis zu sechs Schichten zu Raumfolgen zu arrangiert. Dieser Grundriss zeigt den Auftaktbau der ersten Zeile. Baumwoll-Quartier, Köln, Studie, Somena Holding AG: 2013/14; geplante Fertigstellung: 2022.

An existing former industrial site is to be expanded. Based on an urban development plan by Luca Selva Architekten, the new buildings are to be connected with the protected historic substance of the former cotton bleaching facility. As a response to the existing hall structures, up to six layers are arranged in spatial sequences. This floor plan shows the initial building of the first row. Baumwoll-Quartier, Cologne, study, Somena Holding AG: 2013–2014; scheduled completion: 2022.

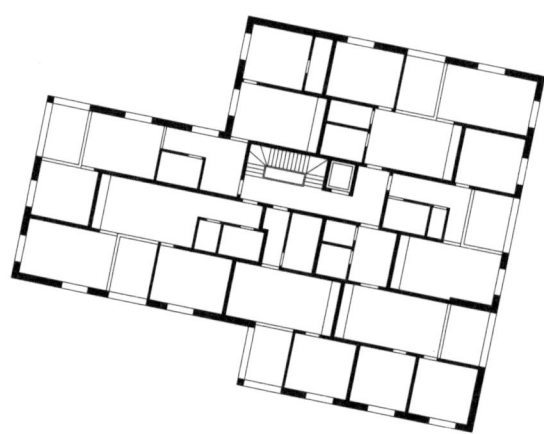

Hier ist der Abschlussbau der zweiten Zeile abgebildet. Baumwoll-Quartier, Köln, Studie, Somena Holding AG: 2013/14; geplante Fertigstellung: 2022.

The final building of the second row is shown here. Baumwoll-Quartier, Cologne, study, Somena Holding AG: 2013–2014; scheduled completion: 2022.

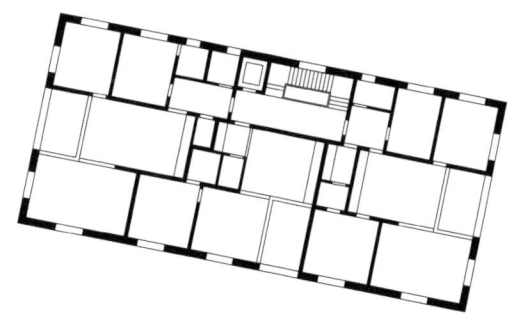

Mit den geschichteten Grundrissen wird auch hier, beim Abschluss der dritten Häuserzeile, das städtebauliche Thema der Reihung aufgenommen und die Nutzung verdichtet. Wohnüberbauung Baumwoll-Quartier, Köln, Studie, Somena Holding AG: 2013/14; geplante Fertigstellung: 2022.

At the end of the third row of the residential buildings is likewise a layered floor plan that incorporates the urban planning theme of the sequence and condenses the occupancy. Baumwoll-Quartier, Cologne, study, Somena Holding AG: 2013–2014; scheduled completion: 2022.

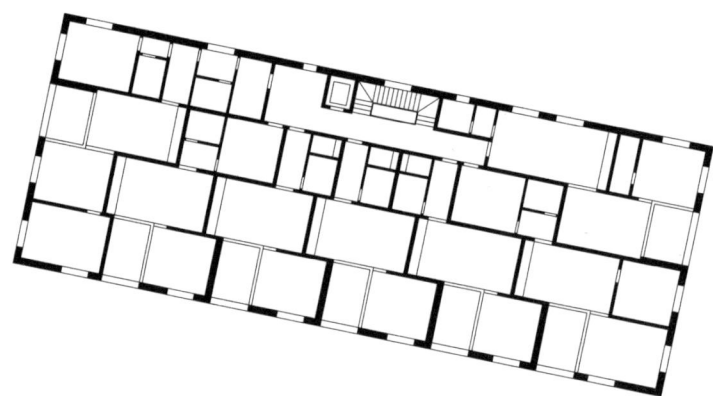

Am Anfang der dritten Zeile steht dieser aus fünf
Schichten konstruierte Bau. Wohnüberbauung
Baumwoll-Quartier, Köln, Studie, Somena Holding AG:
2013/14; geplante Fertigstellung: 2022.

Located at the beginning of the third row,
this building incorporates five spatial layers.
Baumwoll-Quartier, Cologne, study,
Somena Holding AG: 2013–2014; scheduled
completion: 2022.

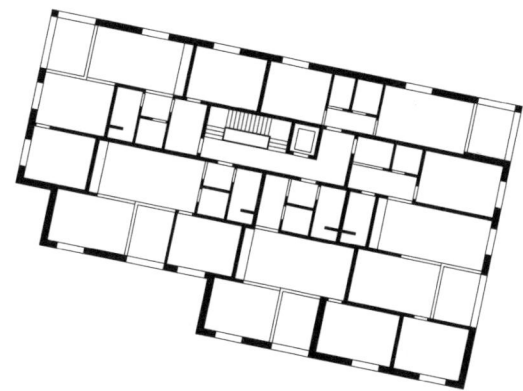

Das Motiv des Peristylhofs fand Eingang in die Palastarchitektur. Im Palazzo Strozzi in Florenz (1539) von Benedetto da Maiano ist der Umgang nur im Piano Nobile verglast, ansonsten offen ausgebildet. Die beiden Treppen verweisen auf die Teilung des Volumens in zwei gleichwertige Wohnungen.

Palazzo Strozzi (1539), Florence, attributed to Simone Pollailo da Sangallo Cronaca and Benedetto da Maiano. The motif of the peristyle courtyard found its way into palace architecture. Only the piano nobile is glazed, while all the remaining parts are open. The two staircases refer to the division of the volume into two equal apartments.

↓

Diese Neubauten sollen Zeilenbauten der 1960er-Jahre ersetzen. Auf lang gestreckten Baufeldern erinnern sie gewissermassen an verdichtete Zeilenbauten. Im Innern formieren sich die gekammerten Grundrisse in zwei bis sechs Schichten. Der Neubau wirkt als zeitgemässe Antwort auf die serielle Mid-Century-Architektur. Ersatzneubauten Heuwinkel- und Eschenstrasse, Allschwil, Studienauftrag im Einladungsverfahren, Graphis Bau + Wohngenossenschaft: 2015.

These new buildings are intended to replace ribbon blocks from the 1960s. Arranged on elongated building plots, they are to some extent reminiscent of the original condensed block forms. In the interior, chambered floor plans are developed in two to six layers. The new building acts as a contemporary answer to typical serial mid-20th-century architecture. Heuwinkelstrasse and Eschenstrasse new buildings, Allschwil, invited study commission, Graphis Bau- + Wohngenossenschaft: 2015.

→

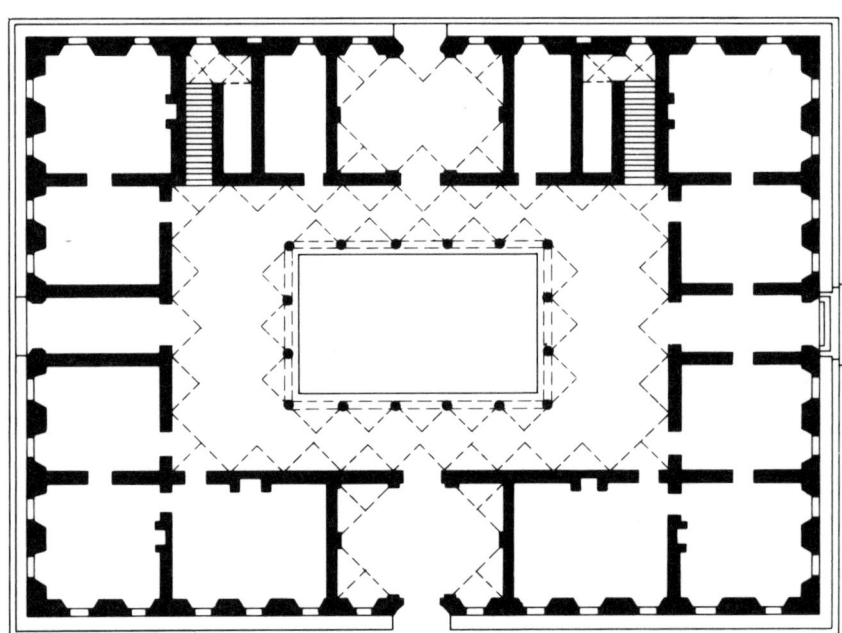

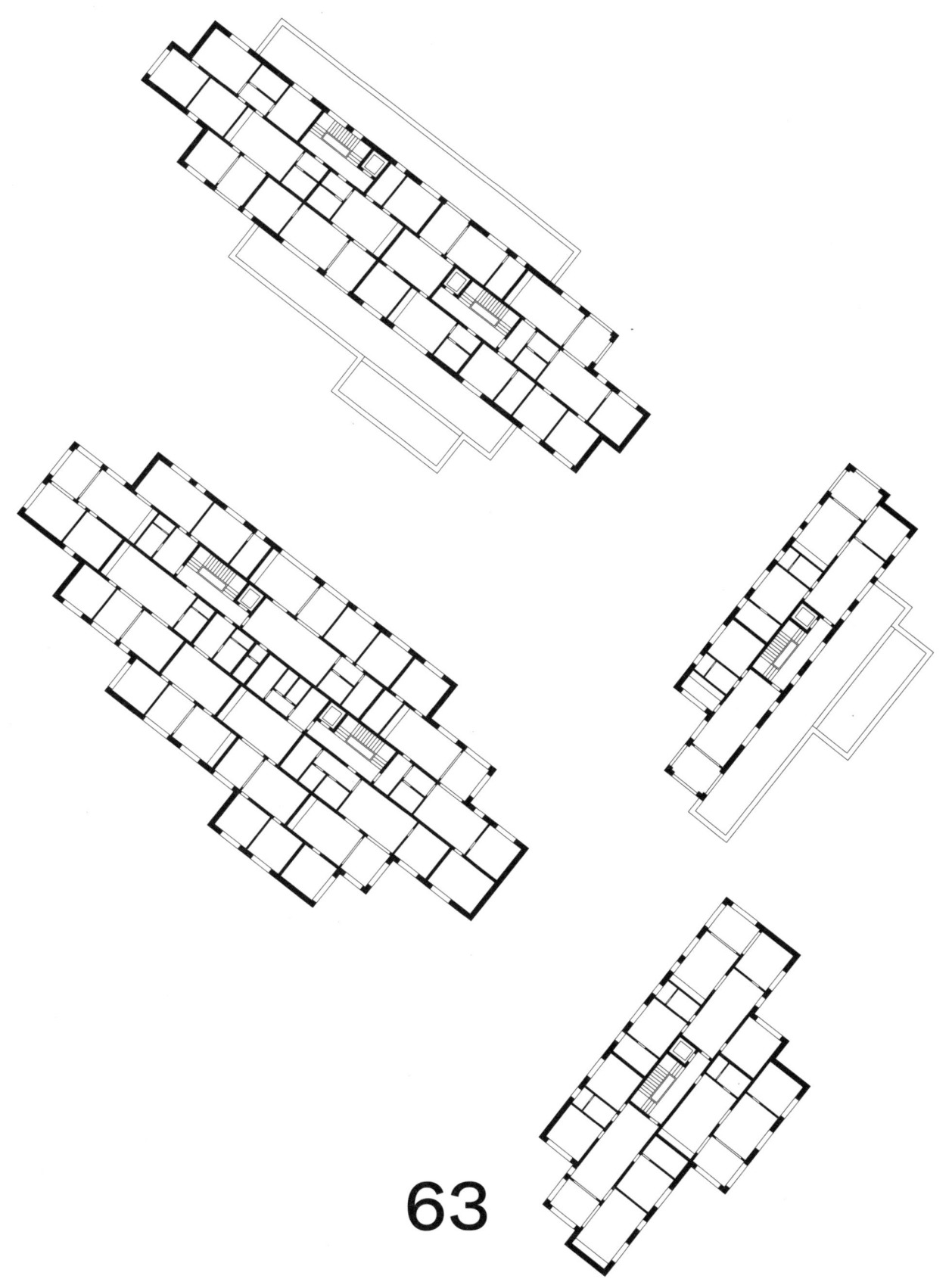

Die Enfilade geht auf das 15. Jahrhundert zurück. Hintereinandergeschaltete, mit Durchgängen in einer Flucht verbundene Räume erzeugen eine perspektivische Wirkung. Erstmalige Anwendung beim Palazzo Venezia in Rom, wo die Zeremonialräume mit der Papstsuite eine räumliche Einheit bilden.

First application of the enfilade, Palazzo Venezia in Rome. Ceremonial rooms and the papal suite form a spatial unit. The enfilade dates back to the 15th century. Placed one after the other and with aligned passageways, the connected spaces generate a perspectival effect.

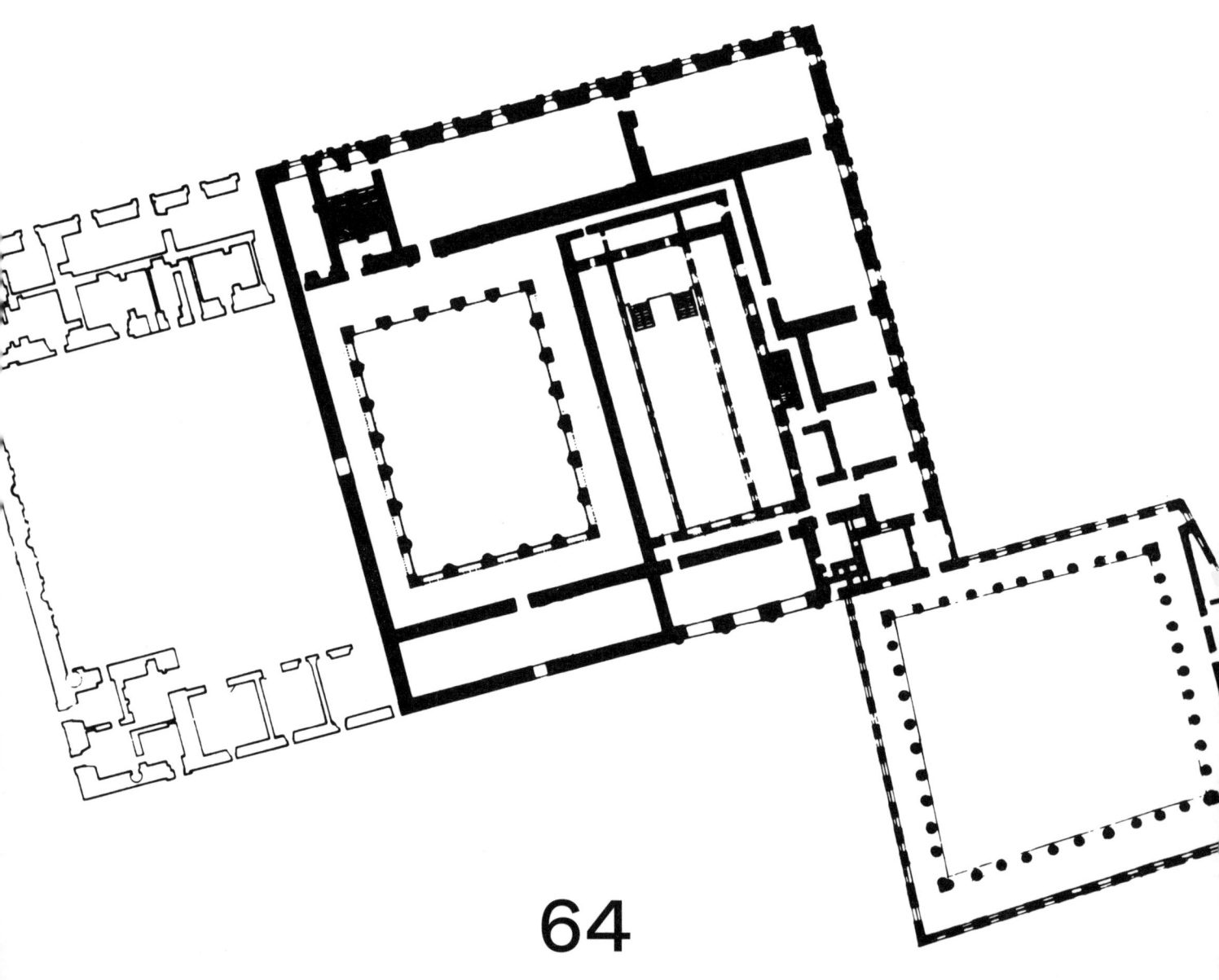

Spiel mit Blickachsen und Durchgängen mittels simpler Reihung der Ausstellungsräume. Zudem sind die Säle und Galerien des Faaborg Museum (1915) in Faaborg von Carl Petersen farblich differenziert gestaltet.

Play with lines of sight and passageways by simple sequencing of exhibition rooms.
In addition, the halls and galleries of the Faaborg Museum (1915) in Faaborg by Carl Petersen are designed in different colors.

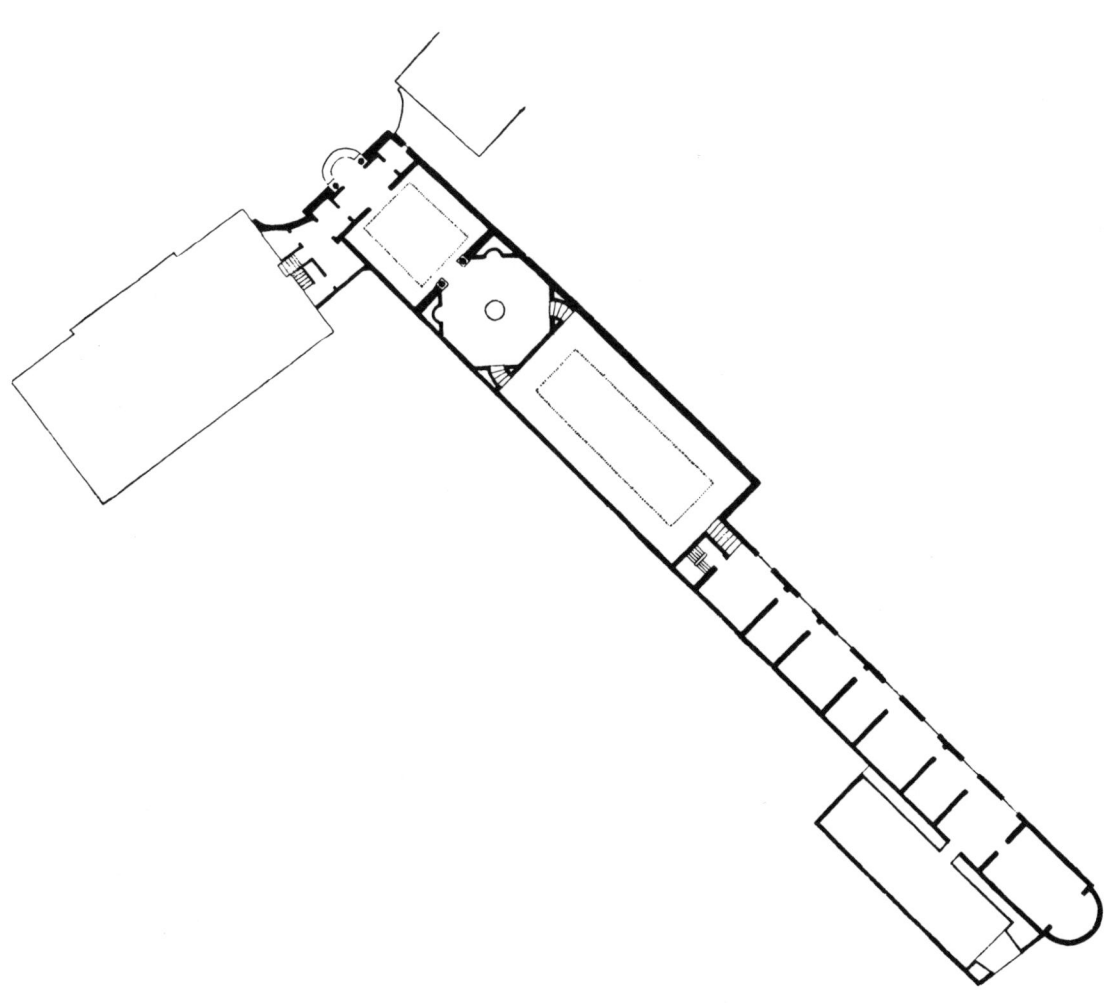

← Plan 57

«Wohnen ist immer eine Summe von Erlebnissen»

Ein Gespräch zwischen
Luca Selva und Patrick Gmür,
moderiert von
Christoph Wieser

CW Luca, wie geht ihr beim Entwerfen vor, wenn ihr mit einem neuen Projekt beginnt?
LS Wir analysieren zuerst die Aufgabe, fragen nach der künftigen Nutzung und versuchen herauszufinden, wie unser Beitrag aussehen könnte: Was wollen wir mit diesem Projekt zeigen, was wollen wir entwickeln, welche Themen wollen wir untersuchen? Wenn wir anfangen, überlegen wir uns, worauf wir Lust haben und welche eigenen Themen in der Luft liegen. Dabei gibt es Wettbewerbe, zu denen man sehr direkt und pragmatisch Zugang hat, und dann gibt es andere Projekte,

"Dwelling Is Always a Sum of Experiences"

An Exchange between
Luca Selva and Patrick Gmür,
Moderated by
Christoph Wieser

CW Luca, how do you go about designing when you start a new project?
LS First we analyze the specified tasks, look into the future usage, and try to find out what our possible contribution might be: What do we want

bei denen sich Themen herauskristallisieren, die im Büro präsent sind. Etwa, wie man mit Grundrissen prinzipiell umgehen könnte, wie man Vorhandenes weiterentwickeln kann. Dabei kommt es vor, dass der Spielraum so klein ist, dass man sich die Welt erst reich machen muss. Es gibt Wettbewerbe, bei denen bis hin zur Lage der Eingänge vieles vorgegeben ist. Und genau dann ist man extrem gefordert herauszufinden, wie man daraus trotzdem etwas machen kann. Viele unserer Projekte sind aus vergleichsweise banalen Ausgangslagen hervorgegangen.

CW Das heisst, ihr eröffnet euch mitunter das Feld über einen geschickten Umgang mit den gegebenen Einschränkungen. Wie ist das bei euch, Patrick?

PG Prinzipiell ist es bei uns das Gleiche. Es geht darum, die Lücken zu finden, gerade im Wohnungsbau, denn hier ist vieles gegeben: In der Küche kocht man, im Schlafzimmer schläft man, im Bad wäscht man sich; nur beim Wohnzimmer ist es ein bisschen unklar, wie man wohnt. Das meiste sind fixe Nutzungen, die werden auch in 50 Jahren noch gesetzt sein. Jetzt geht es darum, wie Luca sagte, eigene Themen zu verfolgen. In dem Punkt gleichen wir uns — wir fragen: Was interessiert uns? Nehmen wir beim Wohnungsbau das Beispiel Lärm: Das ist ein Thema, das man gut verfolgen kann. Die Erkenntnisse aus einem Entwurfsprozess treiben uns ebenfalls weiter. Das ist wie eine eigene Forschung im Büro, das finde ich interessant. Mitunter finden wir die Lücken auch ausserhalb der Wohnung: die Erschliessung, die Materialisierung, die Aussenräume, der Balkon oder das Verhältnis von Innenraum und Aussenraum. Im Mittelpunkt des Entwerfens stehen immer die räumlichen Fragen: Ist es ein offener oder ein geschlossener Grundriss? Wie betrete ich die Wohnung, wie funktioniert die Zirkulation — also wie komme ich zum Beispiel vom Gang in das Wohnzimmer und von dort aus zum WC oder in die Küche? Ich werde da immer grundsätzlich und frage mich: Was will eigentlich das Leben, der Alltag? Das sind die

to demonstrate through this project? What do we want to develop? Which issues do we want to investigate? When we begin, we consider just what we really feel like doing and what themes of our own are "in the air," so to speak. On the one hand, there are competitions that are accessible in a very direct and pragmatic way. And then there are other projects whose themes crystallize out of topics currently being addressed in the office; for example, how to principally deal with floor plans or how to further develop what already exists at hand. However, what can happen is that the leeway is so narrow that first the actual scope has to be enriched. There are competitions where much is predefined, right down to the position of the entrances. And it's precisely in these cases that the challenge is greatest to find out how something can be created out of the situation despite specifications like this. In fact, many of our projects have emerged from comparatively banal initial situations.

CW That means that sometimes you open up a field by dealing skillfully with the given restrictions. How is it with you and your team, Patrick?

PG In principle, it's the same with us. It's about finding the loopholes, especially with residential projects, because that's a remit where a lot of things are predetermined: the kitchen is for cooking, the bedroom for sleeping, the bathroom for bathing; the only space where it's a bit unclear is the living room. Otherwise most usages are fixed, and these will still be set in fifty years. Now, as Luca described, it's about pursuing your own themes. In this sense we're the same—we ask: What are we interested in? With housing, consider, for example, the problem of noise: this is an issue that's easy to pursue. We are also propelled further by discoveries we make during the design process. This is like doing your own research in the office, which I find interesting. Sometimes we also find the opportunities outside the apartment: the overall circulation, materialization, outdoor spaces, balcony, or the relationship

interessanten Fragen beim Wohnungsbau. Es ist eine äusserst wichtige Aufgabe für uns Architekten. Hier können wir uns fast keine Fehler erlauben, weil die Menschen dann in diesen Räumen leben müssen — und zwar nicht nur ein Jahr, sondern wahrscheinlich 50 oder 100 Jahre. Darum muss das äusserst sorgfältig gemacht werden.

CW   Wie macht ihr das, dass ihr trotz enger Vorgaben die eigenen Interessen immer wieder in den Vordergrund schieben könnt?

LS Wenn man in einer Jury sitzt, kann es passieren, dass 30 verschiedene Ansätze auf dem Tisch liegen. Das heisst, wir Architektinnen und Architekten sind offensichtlich stark geprägt von unseren eigenen Erfahrungen, unseren eigenen Interessen. Aber gleichzeitig auch von dem Wunsch, die Dinge ein bisschen weiter zu treiben, die Routinen zu unterlaufen und uns immer wieder neuen Herausforderungen zu stellen. Manchmal braucht es auch mehrere Projekte, um ein Thema bis zu einem befriedigenden Punkt zu diskutieren. Und es gibt Themen, die sich direkt aus dem Ort ergeben. Zum Beispiel beim Neubau des Mehrfamilienhauses an der Meret Oppenheim-Strasse in Basel [Direktauftrag: 2015; Planung und Ausführung: 2015–2019] mit diesem Weitblick auf das Gleisfeld des Bahnhofs SBB. Hier greifen wir mit den anderthalbgeschossigen Räumen ein Thema auf, das nicht wir erfunden haben. Aber es lag auf der Hand, dass wir mit Lösungen experimentieren, denen ganz andere Raumfiguren, auch dreidimensionale, zugrunde liegen. Die Herausforderung liegt darin, sich dem gewählten Thema zu stellen, ihm treu zu bleiben und es auf einen gültigen Stand zu entwickeln. Das ist in Wettbewerben oft gar nicht so einfach, weil da nicht immer die Zeit bleibt, den Beweis für die aufgestellten Thesen zu führen. Wenn man dann am Schluss das Modell anschaut, merkt man: Es ist eine gültige Antwort. Oder man sieht, dass die Dinge noch nicht zusammengekommen sind und sich gegenseitig noch nicht stärken. Dieser Herausforderung, im

between interior and exterior. Spatial questions are always at the center of the design process: Is it an open or a closed ground plan? How do I enter the apartment, how does the circulation work—in other words, how do I get, for example, from the corridor into the living room and from there to the WC or into the kitchen? At this point I always get fundamental and ask myself: What is life, everyday life, about? These are the interesting questions when building housing. It's an extremely important task for us as architects. It's where we can allow ourselves hardly any mistakes because people have to live in these spaces afterward—and not just for a year, but probably rather for fifty or one hundred years. That's why residential projects have to be done with extreme care.

CW   How do you do it so that you can always prioritize your own interests despite narrow stipulations?

LS Serving on a jury, you can have thirty different approaches lying on the table in front of you. This means that as architects we're obviously strongly influenced by our own experiences and our own interests, but at the same time by the desire to push things a bit further, to circumvent routines, and to keep on confronting new challenges. Sometimes it also takes multiple projects to reach a certain satisfactory level in discussing a topic. And there are themes that directly emerge from the location; for instance, during the new residential building on Meret Oppenheim-Strasse in Basel [Direct Commission: 2015, Planning and Execution: 2015–2019] with this wide view across the tracks of the SBB railway station. In this case, using one-and-a-half-story spaces we adopted a topic that we didn't invent ourselves. But naturally we used the opportunity to experiment with solutions based on completely different spatial figures, including three-dimensional ones. The challenge lies in taking a position on the chosen theme, staying true to it, and developing it to a satisfactory level. This is often not so easy in competitions, where there's not always

Entwurfsprozess eine gültige Antwort zu finden, kann man sich durch Routine etwas entziehen. Gerade deshalb müssen wir der Aufgabe immer wieder neu begegnen und Dinge infrage stellen. Das ist auch der Grund, weshalb gerade der Wohnungsbau in der Schweiz ein so hohes Niveau erreicht hat.

PG Christoph, du hast gefragt, wie wir mit Vorgaben umgehen. Ich bin immer froh, wenn wir viele Vorgaben haben, denn dann ist Kreativität gefragt. Das ist ja vielleicht auch der Unterschied zwischen Kunst und Architektur: Der Künstler hat die weisse Leinwand und er hat vielleicht Respekt davor, diese zu füllen. Wir haben wenigstens die Vorgaben. Es gibt bei uns viele Wettbewerbe auf hohem Niveau. Das ist eine Kultur, die wir hochhalten müssen. Und diese Wettbewerbe sind alle gut dokumentiert. Der erste Preis bei einem Wettbewerb bildet die Grundlage für den nächsten. Und bei den Beiträgen, die den zweiten oder dritten Preis bekommen haben, weil die Zeit für den ersten noch nicht so reif war, kann man die Themen und die Vielfalt der Lösungen nachvollziehen. Was wir gemerkt haben: In unserer Wettbewerbskultur muss man sich bewegen, vorwärtsgehen, innovativ sein. Und bei Direktaufträgen muss man noch härter an diesen Themen arbeiten. In unserer Arbeit suchen wir, auch aus Kostengründen, im Moment zum Beispiel nach neuen Ideen für Mehrspänner, für Acht-, Neun-, Zehn- oder auch Zwölfspänner. Wir haben das auch schon in Wettbewerben ausprobiert und sind jedes Mal in der ersten Runde rausgeflogen. Jetzt haben wir einen Direktauftrag, eine Wohnsiedlung in Kloten, bei dem wir diese Frage angehen können. Wir haben noch nie so reibungslos gearbeitet wie dort. Entscheidend ist, wie man das richtige Thema bereits am Anfang findet.

CW Und wie lange man entwirft, bis man sagt: «Jetzt ist es gut, jetzt kommen die Dinge zusammen.» Wann ist dieser Punkt für euch erreicht?

LS Das hat mit der Aufgabenstellung zu tun. Gefragt sind immer bestimmte

enough time to prove the hypotheses that have been formulated. Looking at the model at the end of the process, only then do you realize that it's a compelling solution. That, or it becomes apparent that things have not come together yet and don't yet reinforce each other. This challenge of finding a compelling solution through the design process can be somewhat evaded by routine. So that's exactly why we have to reencounter the task again and again, and question things. That's also precisely the reason why the quality of housing in Switzerland has reached such a high level.

PG Christoph, you asked how we deal with stipulations. I'm always happy when we have a lot of specifications, because it makes creativity all the more necessary. Maybe that's actually the difference between art and architecture. An artist has a blank canvas and she or he maybe feels a respect about filling it. At least we have requirements. There are a lot of high-standard competitions in this country, and it's a culture that we have to maintain. And these competitions are all well documented. The first prize in one competition forms the basis for the next. And the submissions that received the second or third prize—because they weren't yet quite good enough to win—still give you an understanding of the issues and range of possible solutions. What we've noticed is that this competition culture makes it necessary to shift, progress, to be innovative. And with direct commissions it's essential to work even harder on these themes. As an example, for financial reasons we're currently looking in our work for new horizontally arranged multiple-access solutions, involving eight, nine, ten, or even twelve apartments. We've already tried this out in competitions, and each time already got knocked out in the first round. Now we've been given a direct commission, a residential development in Kloten, where we can actually tackle this question. We've never worked so seamlessly as on this project. The key is how to find the right theme from the start.

Grundrisse, bestimmte Grössen und Typen, und wir können gut abschätzen, wie nah wir dem kommen. Aber wonach gefragt wird und woran wir interessiert sind, das ist nicht immer das Gleiche. Deshalb gibt es Projekte, bei denen wir entscheiden, dass wir unser eigenes Thema verfolgen wollen. Dabei riskieren wir mitunter auch, dass der Entwurf nicht mehrheitsfähig ist. Ein Juryprozess, gerade auch im Wohnungsbau, ist oft dominiert von Zurückhaltung, besonders wenn es kommerzielle Investoren sind. Man setzt gerne auf Dinge, die man kennt, die man nachrechnen kann. Der ganze Wohnungsmarkt ist dominiert von Benchmarks. Alle Baukredite werden von den Banken mit dem gleichen Tool auf ihre Wirtschaftlichkeit geprüft. Das führt zu einer gewissen Gleichförmigkeit unter privaten wie auch institutionellen Investoren. Der Markt ist träge. Sobald etwas funktioniert, machen es alle. Das bringt eine gewisse Übersättigung mit sich und umso mehr muss man Alleinstellungsmerkmale entwickeln. Das könnte interessant sein, weil man wieder Häuser mit Charakter entwickeln muss. Wir haben zum Beispiel in Aarburg — wo eigentlich ein Überangebot an Wohnungen besteht — ein Projekt [Gebietsentwicklung Gishalde-Steinbille, Haus A, Aarburg, Studienauftrag: 2014; Planung und Ausführung: 2016–2017 → 57] entwickelt, das ganz anderen Aspekten folgt, beispielsweise durch den Einsatz von Holz und die Orientierung an den Kriterien der 2000-Watt-Gesellschaft. Dort haben wir zum ersten Mal im Wohnungsbau gekammerte Grundrisse tatsächlich bauen können. Das hat mit der alten Lehre zu tun: Wenn der Markt zu einem Nachfragemarkt wird, muss man die Produkte klarer spezifizieren. Und das führt zu Untersuchungen, die für uns interessant sind.

CW Genau. Und Voraussetzung dazu ist natürlich eine genügend grosse Nachfrage. Es gab ja immer wieder Phasen, in denen der Wohnungsbau kaum Thema war.

CW And how long do you keep on with the design stage before saying, "Now it's good, now things are coming together"? When do you reach that point?

LS That has to do with how the task at hand is defined. Certain floor plans, certain sizes and types, are always sought-after, and we can easily estimate how close we are to them. But what's asked for and what we're interested in are not always the same. That's why there are projects where we decide that we want to pursue our own topic. In doing so, we sometimes run the risk that the proposed design solution won't find a majority approval. Jury processes, especially in residential projects, are often swayed by a sense of resistance or caution, especially if commercial investors are involved. People like to back things they already know, that they can reference. The entire housing market is ruled by benchmarks. The banks examine the economic viability of every building loan using the same tool. This leads to a certain uniformity among private as well as institutional investors. The market always lags behind. Once something works, everyone jumps on board, which means there's a certain oversaturation, making it all the more important to develop distinctive features as selling points. This can be interesting because it obliges you to develop housing with character again. For example, in Aarburg—where there's actually a surplus of available apartments—we developed a project [Gishalde-Steinbille Development District, Building A, Aarburg. Study Commission: 2014; Planning and Execution: 2016–2017 → 57] that pursues completely different aspects, such as employing wood and orienting ourselves towards the criteria of the Swiss 2000-Watt Society. This is where we were actually able to build chambered floor plans in housing for the first time. That has to do with the old lesson: in a demand-driven market, you have to make your products stand out more clearly. And that leads to investigations that we find interesting.

LS Als ich in Lausanne studiert habe, gab es dort einen Professor, von dem es hiess, er habe 600 Wohnungen gebaut. Das war für die damalige Zeit sehr viel. Heute hat – etwas zugespitzt formuliert – quasi jedes Büro mit zwei 40-jährigen so viele Wohnungen gebaut. Wir sind jetzt schon bei bald 1000 Wohnungen, die wir gebaut haben oder die in Planung sind; bei den Wettbewerben sind es sicher schon 10 000 oder mehr. Wir sind heute in einem enormen Tempo und einer Dynamik unterwegs – kaum vorstellbar, dass es einmal anders war. Dass sich diese Themen so schnell entwickeln können, hat auch damit zu tun, dass viele Wohnungen produziert werden. Patrick und ich waren beide bei Fierz & Baader Praktikanten: Das renommierte und erfahrene Büro hatte bis dahin überhaupt keine Wohnungen gebaut. Wir bauen da 150 Wohnungen und dort 120 Wohnungen. Das sind immer halbe Quartiere für 500 Menschen. Daraus erwächst auch eine Verantwortung, bei der ich mir nicht sicher bin, ob wir uns alle dessen bewusst sind, was wir da tun. Die entscheidende Frage ist doch: Was hinterlassen wir, wenn der Siedlungsdruck nachlässt? Wir müssen uns immer wieder neu fragen: Wie stellt man Qualität im Wohnungsbau her? Nach der jetzigen Überhitzung wird der Druck wieder zurückgehen. Was hinterlassen wir für diese Zeit? Was ist das für ein Städtebau? Wie sehen die Wohnungen aus? Dabei muss man immer aufpassen, dass man nicht zu früh in eine «Grundrissakrobatik» verfällt. Man muss immer zuerst fragen: Was ist die übergeordnete Qualität? Was ist der Beitrag an die Stadt?

PG Ich glaube, das ist die entscheidende Frage: Was machen wir für die Gesellschaft? Mit Blick auf die Investoren kann man sagen: Das Geld ist derzeit reichlich vorhanden, das muss investiert werden. Ob aber das Bewusstsein für die Qualität und für die übergeordneten gesellschaftlichen Fragen vorhanden ist, da bin ich mir nicht ganz sicher.

CW Auf der Ebene der Stadt ist die räumliche Permanenz sehr hoch. Sie

CW Exactly. And the prerequisite for this, of course, is sufficiently high demand. There have always been phases where the issue of housing architecture has been largely neglected.

LS When I was studying in Lausanne, there was a professor there who was reputed to have built six hundred apartments. For those times that was really a lot. Nowadays—and I'm not simply exaggerating—almost every office with two forty-year-olds has already built that many apartments. At the moment we've reached approximately one thousand apartments that we've either built or are in the planning stage; counting competitions, we'd certainly be at ten thousand or more. Today we're running at an enormously fast and dynamic pace—hard to imagine that things used to be very different. The fact that these themes can evolve so quickly also has to do with the sheer number of apartments that are being produced. Patrick and I were both interns at Fierz & Baader: up to that point this entirely renowned and experienced office had built no apartments whatsoever. Today we build 150 apartments in one place and 120 apartments in another. Imagine! That's a neighborhood big enough for almost five hundred people. But what's emerged out of this situation equally represents a responsibility, whereby I'm not so sure all of us are aware of just quite what we're doing. The key question is: What do we leave behind when housing development pressures subside? We have to keep asking ourselves anew: How do you produce quality in housing? When the currently overheated market ends, demand will go down again. What's the legacy we leave from this period? What kind of urban planning is it? What do the apartments look like? It's essential to be careful not to fall too soon into "floor plan acrobatics." It's always necessary to first ask: What is the overriding quality? What is the contribution to the city?

PG I think that's the crucial question: What are we doing for society? Looking at the investors, you can say that there's a huge amount of money around at the

Zum Rundlauf geschlossen, wird das lineare mit dem radialen Ordnungsprinzip verbunden. Idealtypisch dafür steht die Glyptothek in München von Leo von Klenze, 1830.

Combinination of linear and radial organizational principles in the form of a closed concentric path. An ideal representation of this concept is the Glyptothek (1830), Munich, by Leo von Klenze.

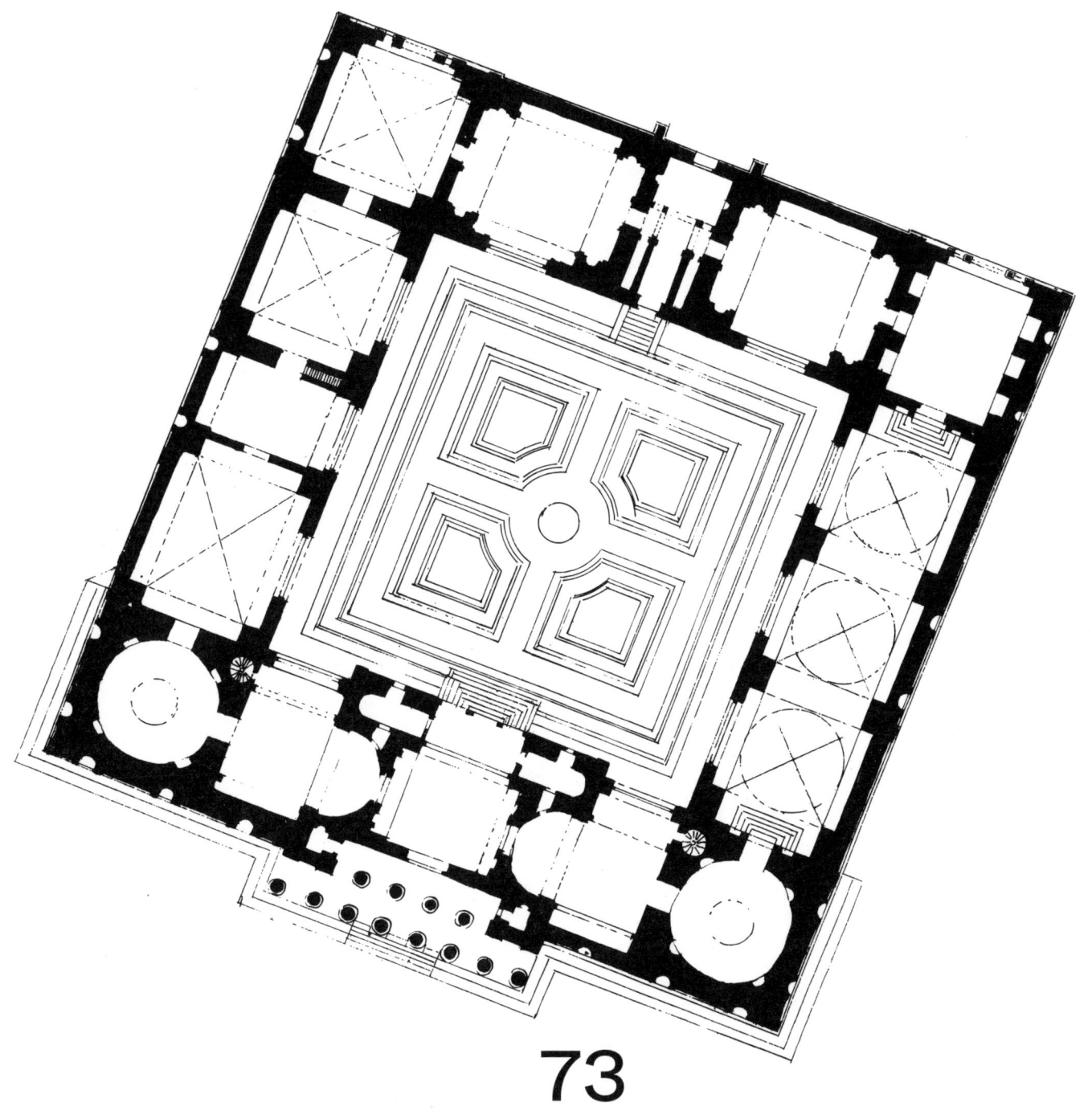

Oberlichtlaternen sind die Voraussetzung für komplexe Kammergrundrisse im Museumsbau. Beim Salisbury Wing der Londoner National Gallery (1991) von Robert Venturi und Denise Scott Brown kommt eine höchst differenzierte Verbindung der Räume hinzu.

Skylights are a prerequisite for complex chambered floor plans in museum architecture. In the Sainsbury Wing (1991) of the National Gallery, London, by Robert Venturi and Denise Scott Brown, the connection between the rooms is highly differentiated.

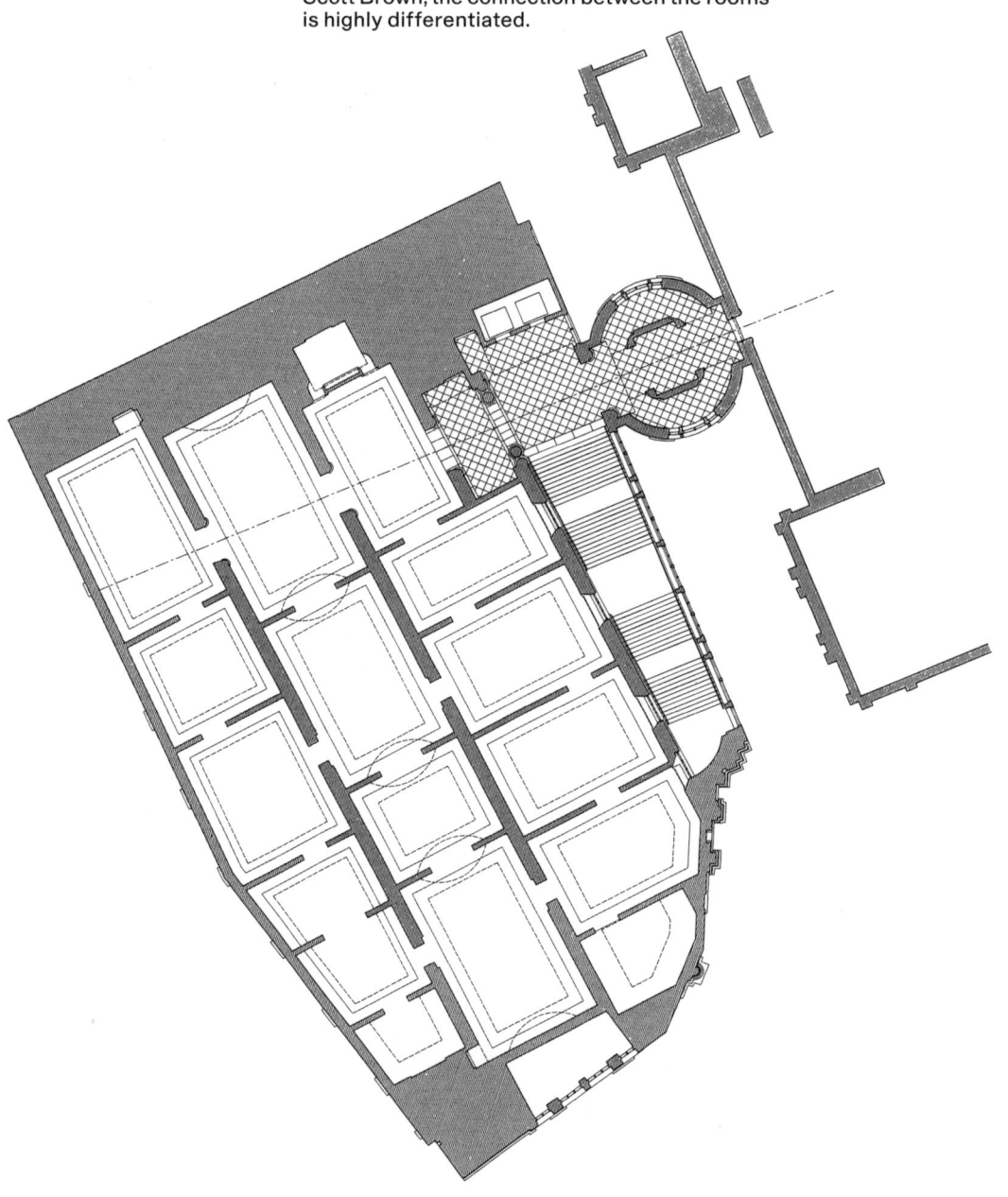

geht weit über das hinaus, was die eigentlichen Gebäude leisten. Das heisst, die Stadträume sind langfristig für die Qualität entscheidend. Gleichzeitig stellt sich die Frage, was die Qualität einer Wohnung ausmacht. Ich finde es interessant, dass du sagst, dass man nicht zu früh in die Grundrissakrobatik gehen soll. Denn mit Blick auf die Entwicklung der letzten Jahre hat man das Gefühl, dass alles ausprobiert wurde. Doch wie weit geht man dabei? Patrick, du hast gesagt, eine Wohnung muss funktionieren, sie muss für den Alltag tauglich sein. Wie macht ihr das?

PG   Wenn die Akrobatik weitergetrieben wird, müssen wir uns fragen, für wen das gemacht wird. Bauen wir für die Architekten oder für die Nutzer? Ich war jetzt ein halbes Jahr in den USA, Saint Louis, Mittlerer Westen. Saint Louis ist in den letzten 50 Jahren um mehr als 60 Prozent geschrumpft. Ich bin extra drei Wochen vorher hingegangen, um eine Wohnung zu suchen. Dann bist du dort und schaust im Internet und du hast nicht eine Wohnung zur Auswahl, sondern Tausende. Und dann noch günstig und zentral gelegen. Vor diesem Hintergrund sieht die Diskussion ganz anders aus. Das können wir uns gar nicht vorstellen. Wir sind in der Schweiz im Architektenparadies. Wir haben im Wohnungsbau das höchste Niveau, das man sich vorstellen kann.

LS   Ähnliches konstatieren wir im Rahmen unserer Arbeit in Deutschland. Wir arbeiten derzeit an einem grösseren Projekt in Köln [Neubau Wohnüberbauung Baumwoll-Quartier, Köln, Studie: 2013/14; Projekt und Ausführung: seit 2016 → 58–61], wo wir eine unter Denkmalschutz stehende ehemalige Fabrikanlage mit einem städtebaulich ganz einfachen Muster erweitern. Dafür haben wir eine Typologie mit gekammerten Grundrissen entwickelt. Als ich das meinen Kölner Kollegen vom BDA vorgestellt habe, meinten sie, das seien die Altbauten. Das war für uns ein Kompliment, weil wir damit aufzeigen, wie man einen Bezug zum Vorhandenen schafft, der das Neue nicht vom Alten abkoppelt.

moment that's begging to be invested. But I'm not so sure there's much awareness about quality and overriding social concerns.

CW   On an urban level, the stakes are very high in terms of spatial permanence. The ramifications go far beyond the actual performance of the individual buildings. In other words, urban spaces determine quality over the long run. At the same time, this raises the question of what constitutes the quality of an apartment. I find it interesting that you warn against resorting to floor plan acrobatics too quickly. Yet considering developments over the past few years, there's a sense that everything has already been tried out. But what and where are the limits? Patrick, you said that an apartment has to function, it has to be suitable for everyday life. How do you do this at your office?

PG   If these acrobatics become more and more contorted, we have to ask ourselves: Who are we doing this for? Are we building for architects or users? Recently I was in the U.S. for six months, in St. Louis in the Midwest. Over the past fifty years St. Louis has shrunk more than 60 percent. I went there specially three weeks in advance to look for an apartment. Then you're there and search the Internet, and you don't have just one free apartment, you have thousands to chose from. And even these are cheap and centrally located. In comparison, the discussion here is completely different. We can't even imagine such a situation. In Switzerland we live in an architect's paradise. We have the highest level of housing construction imaginable.

LS   We've reached similar conclusions in the context of doing projects in Germany. Presently we're working on a larger-scale project in Cologne [New Buildings for a Residential Development, Baumwoll-Quartier, Cologne. Study: 2013–2014; Project and Execution: 2016 onward → 58–61] where we're extending a historically protected existing factory works site by following a very simple urban pattern. Underlying our approach is the development of

Auch wenn nun die Investoren wechseln und Änderungen vorgenommen werden müssten: Es bleibt ein harter Kern übrig, den man nicht verändern kann, weil er eine Logik hat. Wenn das Projekt aber zu stark festgelegt ist, hat man ein Problem mit dem Investor, denn dieser will auf die immer neuen Anforderungen des Marktes reagieren können. Werden die Gene auf die Lebenszeit des Gebäudes festgelegt oder müssen wir Strukturen entwerfen, die sich — wenigstens in der Planungsphase — dem Markt anpassen können? Die Häuser sind inzwischen so hochtechnisiert, dass man eine Wand kaum noch verschieben kann. Das heisst, wir reden über den kurzen Zeitraum vom Wettbewerb bis zum Bezug, wo man eine gewisse Flexibilität hat. Für mich ist das eher eine Scheinflexibilität, um in den Entscheidungsgremien aufseiten der Investoren offener diskutieren zu können.

PG   Die Frage der Flexibilität hat für mich einen direkten Zusammenhang mit der Verantwortung. Die Investoren haben einen Auftrag, sie müssen eine bestimmte Rendite erwirtschaften. Aber ihr Einsatz für eine bestimmte Art von Wohnungen ist gering. Die Firmen, die die ökonomischen Konzepte entwickeln, ändern alle drei Jahre ihre Strategie: Einmal stehen Kleinwohnungen im Fokus, dann wieder braucht es nach ihrer Analyse grosse Wohnungen. Der neueste Trend sind Tiny Houses. Wir haben zurzeit ein solches Projekt in Planung und spüren das grosse Interesse der Medien, aber auch von Kolleginnen und Kollegen und von Menschen, die gerne künftig in einem solchen Tiny House wohnen möchten.

CW   Das Stichwort, das ihr geliefert habt, heisst Struktur. Wie geht ihr damit um? Einerseits gibt es ja den Wunsch der Investoren, ein Gebäude so flexibel wie möglich zu halten. Andererseits sollen gewisse Dinge architektonisch festgelegt werden, was über die Ausbildung der Struktur gut funktioniert.

LS   Das ist richtig. Ich bin geprägt durch die Basler Wohnhäuser Hammerstrasse von Diener & Diener

a typology featuring chambered floor plans. When I presented this to my Cologne colleagues from the BDA, the Association of German Architects, they assumed these were the old buildings. We took this as a compliment, because what we wanted to show with this proposal is how a relationship can be created with what already exists without severing what's new from what's old. Even now, if there would be a change of investors and alterations had to be made, a solid core will survive that can't be changed because an internal logic remains. On the other hand, if a project is laid out too rigidly, this creates a problem with investors because they want to be able to react to ongoing changing market demands. Is the genetic code of a building fixed for its lifespan, or do we have to design structures that can—at least in the planning phase—be adapted to the market? In the meantime buildings have become so high-tech that it's hardly possible anymore to simply shift a wall. In other words, we're talking about the short time span from the competition to moving in that affords a certain degree of flexibility. But in my opinion this is more of a pseudo-flexibility that's simply there to give the investors the secure feeling that there's a scope for discussion within the decision-making bodies.

PG   For me, the question of flexibility is directly related to responsibility. Investors have an obligation to generate a fixed return. But their commitment to a particular type of housing is slight. The firms that develop the economic concepts change their strategy every three years: at one point the focus is on small apartments, then on another occasion, according to their analysis, large apartments are needed. The latest trend is tiny houses. Currently we've got a project like this in the planning phase and have seen the amount of interest it's generating—not only in the media but also from colleagues and people who'd like to live in this kind of tiny house in the future.

CW   The keyword you've given is "structure." How do you treat this?

Architekten (1978–1981). Damals habe ich mein Studium begonnen und zufällig diese Überbauung gesehen. Dann habe ich die Grundrisse studiert: Alles, aber wirklich alles hatte einen Grund! Du konntest daran nichts mehr schieben, jede Tür war am rechten Ort. Alles schrieb sich in eine quadratische Ordnung ein. Mir wurde klar: So müssen Grundrisse sein. Die Glaubwürdigkeit eines Grundrisses entsteht über seine Verbindlichkeit. Die Entwicklung der Tragstruktur hat dann noch zu tun mit dem Fortschreiten des Leichtbaus und natürlich mit dem Budget. Im Laufe der Jahre haben sich die Dinge vielleicht ein bisschen verändert. Aber im Grunde muss man sagen: Im Wohnungsbau wird die Flexibilität durch die Gebäudetechnik eingeschränkt. In einem gelüfteten Haus kannst du keine Wand mehr verschieben. Also muss man darüber nachdenken, ob die Tragstruktur nicht wieder stärker in den Genen des Projekts verankert sein müsste.

PG Ich finde, die Flexibilität wird überschätzt. Die Flexibilität einer Wohnung steht im Widerspruch zu den Realitäten unserer Gesellschaft: Wenn es mir nicht mehr passt, wenn sich die private oder berufliche Situation ändert, dann ziehe ich halt weiter. Es gibt viele Häuser, die arbeiten mit einer fixen Struktur, so wie wir bei der Wohnüberbauung Paul-Clairmont-Strasse in Zürich [Einladungswettbewerb, 1. Preis: 2000; Ausführung: 2003–2006]. Prägend sind deren zweigeschossige Balkone. Wir haben anderthalb Jahre versucht, diesen Code zu entschlüsseln. Und als wir ihn hatten, konnte man daran nichts mehr ändern. Solche Häuser sind stark, sie prägen den Bestand und sie sollen weiter bestehen.

CW Aus meiner Sicht geht ihr sehr unterschiedlich mit der Struktur um. Luca, in euren Arbeiten ist die Kammerung sehr präsent. Und bei euch, Patrick, sehe ich viel stärker das Thema Stützen/Platte. Sind das Vorlieben oder entwickelt ihr eure Projekte stärker über spezifische Grundrisse und Typologien?

PG Ich würde mich da nicht so streng einordnen. Spannend ist doch, in ein

On the one hand, investors want to keep a building as flexible as possible. On the other, certain items have to be architecturally determined, and must function well however the structure is articulated.

LS That's right. My approach has been influenced by the Hammerstrasse housing development in Basel, conceived and built by Diener & Diener Architekten from 1978 to 1981. At the time I'd just started my studies and happened to see the project by chance. I then studied the floor plans—everything, I mean really everything, had a reason! There wasn't anything in them that could be shifted. Every door was in the right place. Everything had been inscribed in a quadratic arrangement. It became clear to me: this is how floor plans ought to be. The credibility of a floor plan arises from its irrevocability. Back then the development of the load-bearing structure still had to do with advances in lightweight construction and, naturally, with the budget. Over the years maybe things have slightly changed, but basically it goes without saying that flexibility in residential construction is limited by building technology. In a mechanically ventilated building it's no longer possible to move a wall. So it's necessary to think about whether the load-bearing structure shouldn't be more firmly anchored in the genes of a project.

PG I find flexibility overrated. The flexibility of an apartment contradicts the realities of our society. If it no longer suits me, if my private or professional situation changes, then I just move on. There are numerous buildings that work with a fixed structure, like we did at the Paul-Clairmont-Strasse residential development in Zurich [Invited Competition, First Prize: 2000; Execution: 2003–2006]. In this case, the two-story balconies shaped the overall project. We tried for one and a half years to decipher this code. And once we'd cracked it, nothing more could be changed. Buildings like this are powerful: they shape their existing architectural surroundings, and they

Gebäude das Maximum an Wohnungen hineinzubekommen. Mitunter ist es so wie Kofferpacken. Wenn ich am Ende auch noch die Socken unterbekomme, ist es ideal gelaufen. Das macht mir Freude! Und wenn ich Themen finde zur Struktur, zum Raum und zum Aussenraum, dann ist das toll. Man kann die Architektur aus dem Ort entwickeln oder man gibt sich Themen: etwa den zweigeschossigen Balkon. Wobei wir dort nicht gesagt haben: «Wir brauchen einen zweigeschossigen Balkon.» Wir haben gesagt: «Jetzt machen wir mal eine Wohnung mit einem anständigen Balkon.» Und da haben wir bald gemerkt, dass die Belichtung ein Problem wird. Dann ging die Forschung anhand ganz einfacher Fragestellungen weiter: Jetzt machen wir mal tiefe Grundrisse, welches Potenzial haben die? Wir arbeiten weniger nach irgendeinem Prinzip, sondern widmen uns Ideen und der Lust, etwas Neues auszuprobieren.

CW Aber mehrheitlich sind es doch offene, fliessende Räume, die eure Projekte auszeichnen. Und bei euch, Luca, sind die Räume tendenziell stärker gefasst, stehen aber in enger Beziehung zueinander. Wie kommt es, dass euch die Kammerung so fasziniert?

LS Ich kann beschreiben, wie sich das bürobiografisch entwickelt hat. 2010 sind wir eingeladen worden an den Wohnbauwettbewerb für die Siedlung Sandfelsen in Erlenbach. Dort gab es zwei Baufelder in der Grösse 12 × 25 Meter. Es galt einfach, diese Felder aufzufüllen. Für uns war das nicht Herausforderung genug, wir wollten etwas Neues untersuchen. Wir haben in der Folge zwei Typen erarbeitet, einmal mit der Tragstruktur in Längs- und einmal in Querrichtung, und haben leichte Trennwände und Einbauten in der Gegenrichtung dazwischen eingestellt. Damit konnten wir unglaublich interessante Grundrisse entwickeln. Wir konnten die Räume unhierarchisch miteinander verbinden und zugleich die Tiefe bewältigen. Und wir konnten mit eingezogenen Loggien das natürliche Licht sehr gut in die Wohnungen bringen. Auf diese Weise haben wir

should continue to be where they are and do what they do.

CW From my point of view, the two of you deal very differently with structure. Luca, in your projects, working with chambering is very present. And with you, Patrick, I see the theme of supports and slabs is much stronger. Are these preferences or do you develop your projects more intensely based on specific floor plans and typologies?

PG I wouldn't necessarily classify myself in terms of such strict categories. But it's compelling to manage to get the maximum number of apartments into a building. Sometimes it's like packing a suitcase. When I'm almost done, if I can still squeeze in my socks then things have gone perfectly. It gives me pleasure! And when I find themes related to structure, space, and outdoor space, well that's great. The architecture can be developed out of the site or themes can be pursued; for example, the two-story balcony. However, in this case we didn't say, "We need a two-story balcony." Instead we said, "Let's make an apartment with a decent balcony," and then we soon realized that getting enough daylight into the interior was going to be a problem. From there we re-intensified our research based on exploring very simple questions: Now if we make deep floor plans, what potential do they have? Rather than following some principle or another, we commit ourselves to ideas and the desire to try out something new.

CW But nevertheless, what predominantly characterize your projects are open, flowing spaces. And with your office's work, Luca, while the spaces tend to be more contained, they are still interrelated. How did it come about that chambering is such a fascination for you and your team?

LS I can describe how this evolved in terms of the history of the office. In 2010 we were invited to take part in the housing competition for the Sandfelsen scheme in Erlenbach. Within the overall development area there were two designated building lots measuring 12 meters by 25 meters. The job was simply to fill

eine reiche Welt geschaffen. Was uns in diesem Wettbewerb jedoch überhaupt nicht gelungen ist, ist die Skalierung. Die Wohnungen waren viel zu gross. Die Jury hat die Qualität gewürdigt, zugleich aber festgestellt, dass die Wohnungsgrössen untauglich seien → 6. Wir haben über viele Wettbewerbe und Bauprojekte hinweg an diesem Thema weitergearbeitet, zuletzt etwa beim bereits genannten Projekt in Köln, wo wir die gleichen Prinzipien anwendeten. Dabei haben wir nach und nach entdeckt, dass man sehr viele Spielarten und Freiheiten hat. In Köln hat der Investor uns dazu aufgefordert, ihn zu überzeugen, dass diese Grundrisse intelligent seien. Wir haben uns mit ihm verschiedene Beispiele im Büro angeschaut, sind nach Aarburg gefahren und haben uns die dortigen Bauten angesehen → 57. Das hat den Investor überzeugt, er hat unsere Grundrisse angenommen. In dieser speziellen Lage in Köln kann er nun etwas Besonderes anbieten. Die Kammerung kann Tiefe bewältigen, obwohl die Flächen relativ knapp sind. Die Räume können unterschiedlich genutzt werden und es gibt viel Transparenz und damit Blickachsen in der Wohnung → 58–61. Wir haben also «in ein Gespräch gefunden». Wir wünschen uns, dass man herausfindet, weshalb und wie unsere Grundrisse funktionieren. Das System scheint zwar starr, ist aber mit Qualität verbunden. Ein Beispiel dafür: Ich wohne mit meiner Familie mit einer Terrasse gegen Westen und ohne Gegenüber. Da gibt es um Weihnachten herum Tage, an denen die Sonne 12 oder 14 Meter tief in die Wohnung scheint und dort ein Bild beleuchtet. Das macht mich glücklich. Solche Details tragen wesentlich zur Qualität einer Wohnung bei und können sich mit den Emotionen der Menschen verbinden. Ich glaube, Wohnen ist immer eine Summe von Erlebnissen. Mehrspännige Grundrisse beispielsweise führen zu grossen Treppenhäusern, zu repräsentativen Räumen, die eigentlich wunderbar sind. Es gibt somit neben dem ökonomischen einen räumlichen Mehrwert.

in these two lots. For us that wasn't enough of a challenge: we wanted to explore something new. Subsequently we worked out two types: one with the load-bearing structure oriented lengthwise, and one with it crosswise, placing light partition walls and built-in components in between in the opposite directions. This made it possible for us to create incredibly interesting floor plans. We were able to connect the spaces in a non-hierarchical way and at the same time master the depth. And using recessed loggias we were able to successfully bring daylight into the apartments. By following this approach we created a really rich environment. However, what we didn't succeed with at all in this competition was the sizing; in other words, the apartments were much too big. The jury acknowledged the high quality at the same time as declaring that the apartment sizes were unsuitable → 6. We've continued working on this theme through many competitions and building projects, most recently in the project in Cologne I mentioned, where we applied the same principles. In doing so, we gradually discovered just how much variety and scope was truly available. In Cologne, the investor challenged us to convince him that our floor plans were intelligent. We looked at different examples with him in the office and then traveled to Aarburg to look at the buildings there → 57. The investor found it so convincing that he agreed to our floor plans. Now, at this special location in Cologne he can offer something exceptional. The chambering successfully masters the depth even though the floor areas are relatively constrained. The spaces can be used in different ways and there is a lot of transparency, which establishes visual axes in the apartment → 58–61. In short, we managed to establish what you'd call a "fruitful dialog." We really want others to find out why and how our floor plans work. The system may seem rather rigid, but it's tied to quality. An example of what I mean by this: I live with my family with a terrace facing west with no one opposite. There

Die Erschliessungsflächen sind den Zimmern zugeschlagen. Damit kann die Wohnung klein gehalten werden, ohne dass ein Gefühl von Enge entsteht. Typengrundriss aus einem Buch zum Sozialen Wohnungs- und Siedlungsbau der Schweiz im Zweiten Weltkrieg.

Floor plan type from a book about social housing and settlements in Switzerland during World War II. Circulation areas are added to the rooms in order to make the apartment small without creating a feeling of confinement.

CW   Räumlicher, atmosphärischer und typologischer Reichtum ist bei euch, Patrick, ebenfalls ein grosses Thema. Die Überbauung James in Zürich [Wettbewerb: 2001; Ausführung: 2004–2009] beispielsweise oder andere Projekte überraschen mit einer Vielzahl unterschiedlich geschnittener Wohnungen. Heisst das, dass ihr nicht über ein Ordnungsprinzip wie die Kammerung, sondern über die Varianz der Typologie versucht, diesen von Luca beschriebenen Reichtum zu erzeugen?

PG   Ja, die Vielfalt der Typologie ist für uns ein wichtiges Mittel. Die Frage des Reichtums stellt sich aber auch im Leben: Jedes kann reich sein und jedes ist anders. So ist das auch bei Wohnungen. Sie müssen nicht alle gleich sein. Bei uns steht zudem der fliessende Raum im Vordergrund und nicht die Kammerung. Wir hatten damit einfach noch keinen Erfolg, ein dritter Preis war bislang die beste Platzierung. Es ist anspruchsvoll, den Investor davon zu überzeugen, dass in die Tiefe gestaffelte Räume funktionieren.

LS   Und sie funktionieren wirklich gut!

PG   Aber der Investor muss daran glauben oder eben die Jury. Für das Zwhatt-Areal in Regensdorf [Einladungswettbewerb: 2019] haben wir genau diesen Typ entwickelt — mit dem Wohnen in der zweiten Reihe in einem Hochhaus, wo man sowieso nie Belichtungsprobleme hat, weil das Gegenüber fehlt. Aber sie haben uns nicht geglaubt. Damit kommen wir zu einem weiteren Thema: Unsere Wettbewerbskultur ist ein wesentlicher Garant für Innovation im Wohnungsbau. Entweder erforscht das eigene Büro in mehreren Wettbewerbsverfahren ein spezifisches Thema oder Kolleginnen und Kollegen erbringen mit ihren Bauten den Nachweis, dass es funktioniert. Gebaute Beispiele, die trotz grosser Widerstände und weiter Wege realisiert werden und auf die man sich als Referenz beziehen kann, sind wichtig. Wenn der Investor solche Gebäude sieht, glaubt er es meist auch. Und die Kammergrundrisse sind ein unendlich weites und interessantes Feld.

are days around Christmas when the sun shines 12 or 14 meters deep into the apartment and illuminates a picture hanging there. That makes me happy. Details like this contribute significantly to the quality of an apartment and can connect with people's feelings. I think dwelling is always a sum of experiences. Multi-access circulation floor plans, for instance, lead to large staircases, to representative spaces that are actually wonderful. Not only does this give added economic value but added spatial value too.

CW   Patrick, spatial, atmospheric, and typological richness is also an important concern of yours. For example, the James development project in Zurich [Competition: 2001; Execution: 2004–2009], or other projects, are surprising in their multitude of differently laid-out apartments. Does that mean that you try to create the richness described by Luca not through a principle of organization, such as chambering, but rather through varying the typology?

PG   Yes, diversity of typology is an important method for us. But the question of richness also occurs in life. Everyone can be rich and everyone is different. The same applies to apartments. They don't all have to be identical. In addition, for us flowing space is a priority, not chambering. We just haven't had any success with it yet. Up to now, a third prize was as far as we've got. It is difficult to convince an investor that deeply staggered spaces can indeed work.

LS   And they do function really well!

PG   But the investor has to believe in it, or the jury. For the Zwhatt-Areal in Regensdorf [Invited Competition: 2019] we developed precisely this version, with the dwellings set back, so to say, in the second row in a high-rise, and where there are never problems with daylight exposure anyway because there aren't any buildings opposite. But they didn't believe us. This brings us to a further issue. Our culture of competitions essentially ensures innovation in housing. Either your own office does research about a specific theme while

CW Was mich daran fasziniert, ist die Tatsache, dass Kammergrundrisse auf dem Plan etwas Stempelartiges, Starres haben. Aber in Wirklichkeit, im Erleben, in den Räumen selbst, ist der Grundriss gar nicht das Prägende. Dort sind es immer die Raumbezüge, die Diagonalen. Wie arbeitet ihr mit den Diagonalen? Wie ordnet ihr die Räume zueinander an, wie organisiert ihr die Verbindungen zwischen den Zimmern, die ja von zentraler Bedeutung sind?

LS Das Thema beschäftigt uns seit dem ersten Wettbewerb, den wir gewonnen haben, den für das Kaltbrunnen-Schulhaus [Neubau Kaltbrunnen-Schulhaus, Basel, Wettbewerb 1993, 1. Preis; Projekt und Ausführung: 1994–1996 → 12]. Zu dessen Kontext gehört die Katholische Allerheiligen-Kirche von Hermann Baur 1947 und ein bestehendes Schulhaus von Giovanni Panozzo aus den frühen 1950er-Jahren, für das eine Erweiterung darzustellen war. Wir haben uns quer zur Kirche gesetzt und mit den offenen Diagonalen gespielt. Anhand dieser rechtwinkligen Setzung haben wir gemerkt, dass genau darin der Reichtum liegt. Beim Densa-Areal [Wohnüberbauung Densa Park, Basel, Wettbewerb: 2008; Planung und Ausführung: 2008–2012] haben wir in der Stellung der Volumen auch damit gearbeitet. Dort haben wir zwei Gebäude gesetzt, die miteinander Räume bilden, aber zugleich über die offenen Diagonalen immer wieder neue Bezüge herstellen. Und das ist das Entscheidende: wie das Auge geführt wird. So ist das zum Beispiel auch in Aarburg. Die Frage ist immer: Wo hast du eine «gute» Wand? Wo hängt das Bild, wo steht das Möbel? Gute Wände gibt es in den Wohnungen von heute praktisch nicht mehr.

PG Du sprichst von der guten Wand, wir sprechen von der Kuschelecke, in der man sich sein Nest bauen kann, wo man geschützt ist und sich zum Beispiel einander den Tag erzählen kann.

LS Es ist ja auch ein bisschen die Sehnsucht, dass die Dinge eine Logik haben müssen und auch eine Stärke bekommen, wenn sie mehr als einen participating in several competitions or buildings by other colleagues prove that it works. Built examples that have been completed despite huge objections and torturous proceedings, and which can therefore be given as a reference, are vital. When investors see such buildings, they usually believe it too. And chambered floor plans are an infinitely wide and interesting field.

CW What fascinates me is the fact that when viewed in layout, chambered floor plans have something compartmental or rigid about them. But in reality, with lived experience, actually being in the spaces, the floor plan is not domineering at all. Being there, it's always about the spatial interrelationships, the diagonals. How do you work with the diagonals? How do you arrange the spaces in relation to one another? How do you organize the connections between the rooms, which indeed are highly significant?

LS We've been dealing with this theme since the first competition we won, the one for the new Kaltbrunnen Schoolhouse in Basel [Competition, First Prize, 1993; Project and Execution: 1994–1996 → 12]. The context includes the Catholic All Saints Church by Hermann Baur from 1947 and an existing school building by Giovanni Panozzo from the early 1950s, which needed to be enlarged. We decided to position our project obliquely to the church and then played with the open diagonals that resulted. By examining this right-angled placement, we noticed that this situation presented the greatest potential. With the Densa-Areal [Densa Park Residential Development, Basel. Competition: 2008; Planning and Execution: 2008–2012] we also worked on this through the positioning of the volumes. There we placed two buildings so that they not only form spaces with each other but simultaneously and continuously create new correlations via the open diagonals. And that's what's critical: how the eye is guided. This is also the case, for instance, in Aarburg. The question is always: Where do you have a "correct wall"? Where is

Grund haben. Die Wand ist Teil eines Trag- und Raumsystems. Meist arbeiten wir bei Kammergrundrissen mit vier Schichten, mit mehr wird es schwierig, aber es funktioniert immer noch. Kommt die fünfte Schicht hinzu, muss man das Ganze als Punkthaus aufbauen. Für einen Wettbewerb in Allschwil [Ersatzneubauten Heuwinkelstrasse, 2005 → 63] oder im Baumwoll-Quartier in Köln [2015–2022 → 58–61] haben wir sogar mit sechs Schichten gearbeitet.

PG Das Kammern der Grundrisse hat immer etwas mit der Verteilung der Funktionen zu tun: Wo schläft man, wo kocht man, wo wohnt man?

LS Genau. Und es ist unhierarchisch.

PG Richtig. Eine Wohnung zu organisieren, die in einer Ecke liegt, ist einfach, weil es kein Belichtungsproblem gibt. Anders ist es, wenn die Räume sich in die Tiefe entwickeln. Wir haben ein Haus an der Imbisbühlstrasse in Zürich gebaut [Einladungswettbewerb: 2003; Ausführung: 2007/08], das diese Themen *in extenso* abbildet.

CW Beim Kammergrundriss sind somit das Serielle, die Repetition, die Schichtung wichtige Aspekte. Das zeigt eine gewisse Nähe zum Strukturalismus. Dennoch meine ich, dass eure Projekte, Luca, nicht strukturalistisch gedacht sind, sondern auf der Beziehung der Räume zueinander aufbauen.

PG Das Prinzip geht von den Räumen aus, ist aber auch sonst sehr schlau: Wir haben geringe Spannweiten und andere Vorteile, die das Bauen einfacher machen.

CW Das ist ja der Grund, weshalb man früher nahezu immer gekammerte Grundrisse verwendet hat. Man hat über die ökonomisch und konstruktiv sinnvolle Spannweite die Grösse der Räume definiert. Ist die Ökonomie der Mittel für euch heute auch ein Thema, das mit dieser Typologie verbunden ist?

PG Die Ökonomie ist gerade im Wohnungsbau immer ein Thema. Hier geht es darum, die Lücke zu finden, etwas zu entwerfen, das nicht kostentreibend ist. Eine einfache Statik ist immer gut. Daran haben wir uns beispielsweise bei

the picture hung? Where do you put the furniture? In today's apartments, there are practically no correct walls anymore.

PG You call it the correct wall, whereas we speak about the cozy corner in which you can build your nest, where you feel protected and you can tell each other, for instance, about how the day went.

LS There's also a bit of the longing that things should have a certain logic and also resonate more when they have more than one reason. The wall is part of a structural-support and spatial system. When we work with chambered floor plans, we usually deal with four layers. With more, it becomes difficult, but it still functions. Adding a fifth layer, the whole thing has to be arranged as a point-block building. For the competitions in Allschwil [Heuwinkelstrasse, replacement buildings: 2005 → 63] and for the Baumwoll-Quartier in Cologne [commenced 2015; scheduled completion 2022 → 58–61] we even worked with six layers.

PG The chambering of the floor plan always has something to do with the distribution of functions: Where do you sleep? Where do you cook? Where is the area for lounging or social activities?

LS Exactly! And it's non-hierarchical.

PG Right. Organizing an apartment situated on a corner is easy, because there's no problem with daylight exposure. It's different when spaces are developed in depth. We built a house on Imbisbühlstrasse in Zurich [Invited Competition: 2003; Execution: 2007–2008] that depicts these themes *in extenso*.

CW Important aspects of the chambered floor plan are seriality, repetition, and layering. This approximates features of Structuralism. Nevertheless, I think that your projects, Luca, are not intended to be Structuralist but are rooted in the interrelationship between the spaces.

PG The principle proceeds from the spaces, but it's also very clever in other respects: we have short spans and other advantages that make construction easier.

den zwei Wohnhäusern für Studierende und das Personal des Universitätsspitals in Zürich [Studienauftrag: 2012; Planung und Ausführung: 2013–2018] gehalten, die sehr kostengünstig sein mussten. Wir suchen immer nach Möglichkeiten, Geld zu sparen, ohne dass man es sieht. Das ist die grosse Kunst beim Wohnungsbau.

LS Der entscheidende Punkt ist, ob man daran glaubt, in der zweiten Reihe wohnen zu können. Man muss aber aufpassen, dass das nicht zu etwas Zynischem wird. Der Kammergrundriss darf kein Instrument werden, um allein aus ökonomischen Gründen Flächen zu sparen, sondern soll einen räumlichen Gewinn abwerfen. Mir hat einmal ein Investor gesagt: «Wenn man die Zitrone auspressen will, dann helfen einem immer die Architekten, denn sie sind so innovativ, dass sie auch in dieser Hinsicht nochmal optimieren können.» Wir müssen uns immer wieder die Frage stellen: Was hat das mit dem richtigen Leben zu tun, wie ist das in 20 und in 30 Jahren? Ich habe zum Beispiel immer in Wohnungen gewohnt, schon als Kind. Und dann kam irgendwann mal die Nachbarwohnung hinzu, dann sind es zwei Wohnungen gewesen, horizontal verbunden. Als ich dann mit meiner Familie in einem Baumgartner-Haus wohnte, hatten wir die Gelegenheit, unsere Wohnung und die darüber liegende zu kaufen. Und jetzt wohne ich auch wieder in einer, die aus zwei zuvor getrennten Wohnungen entstand. Ich behaupte, es gibt Lebenserfahrungen, die sich verdichten und die man adaptiert, weil sie gut waren.

PG Du sprichst von der eigenen Wohnbiografie. Man kann es auch anders formulieren: Es ist das, was man am besten kennt und einem vertraut ist. Ich würde zum Beispiel gern Flughäfen bauen, aber ich kann da meine Erfahrung nicht so gut einbringen. Beim Wohnen ist das anders. Das Wohnen, die eigene Wohnerfahrung, das hat mich immer interessiert. Ich bin in einem Doppelhaus aufgewachsen, das mein Vater im Sinne von Le Corbusier gebaut hat, alles in Sichtbeton.

CW That's the reason why chambered floor plans were almost always used in the past. The size of the spaces was defined using the economically and constructively appropriate span. Is this economy of means that this typology entails also a theme for you in the present?

PG Right now being economical is always an issue, especially in residential projects. The point here is to find the loopholes, to design something that doesn't increase costs. A simple structural system is always a good idea. We adhered to this maxim, for instance, in two residential buildings we completed for the students and staff of the University Hospital Zurich [Study Commission: 2012; Planning and Execution: 2013–2018], which had to be very economical. We're always looking for ways to save money without it being visible. That's the great art of doing housing.

LS The crucial point is whether you believe it's possible to live one layer back. But it's important to be careful that this doesn't become something cynical. The chambered floor plan shouldn't become an instrument to save space for economic reasons alone, but ought to be a means to gain space. An investor once told me that if you want to squeeze the lemon dry, architects are always helpful because in this respect they're so innovative they can always find a way to further optimize. We have to keep asking ourselves: "What does this have to do with real life? What will this be like in twenty and in thirty years from now?" For example, I've always lived in an apartment, even as a child. And then at some point the apartment next door was added onto it—then there were two apartments connected horizontally. When I later lived with my family in a house built by Wilhelm Emil Baumgartner, we had the opportunity to buy our apartment and the one above it. And now I'm living once again in an apartment created from two previously separate ones. My conclusion is that sometimes life's experiences coalesce and you then adapt them, precisely because they were good.

Plan 105/106 →

Als ich in die Schule kam und meine Freundinnen und Freunde nach Hause eingeladen habe, sagten sie: «Du bist so ein Armer, du wohnst noch auf der Baustelle.» Das hat mich sehr beschäftigt. Ich glaube, das war einer der Gründe, warum ich mich noch heute mit dem Wohnen intensiv befasse – wo fühle ich mich wohl, wie erzeuge ich Gemütlichkeit und so weiter. Damit beantworte ich auch deine ursprüngliche Frage, wie wir vorgehen. Das ist etwas, das Luca und mich unbewusst verbindet: Wir beziehen uns immer wieder auf die eigenen Erfahrungen. Christoph, du hast ja vom Kalibrieren gesprochen und davon, wie man zur Massstäblichkeit kommt. Ich stelle fest, dass manche Architektinnen und Architekten keine Ahnung mehr haben, wie gross ein Tisch oder wie hoch eine Küchenablage sein sollte. Ihnen fehlt der Bezug zu Dimensionen. Vielleicht hat dies mit der Art des Zeichnens am Computer zu tun. Für uns ist es ein Privileg, dass wir uns diese Erfahrung erarbeitet haben. Vielleicht ist das auch ein bisschen das Geheimnis unseres Erfolgs. Du hast von der Diagonalen gesprochen und all diesen Dingen – dafür muss man zuerst einmal die Basis haben. Wenn ich dein Werk verfolge, Luca, spüre ich, wie diese Erfahrung hineinkommt, dieser Reichtum. Und das ist immer das Gute, wenn man selber baut: Nach der Fertigstellung eines Wohnungsbaus besuche ist diesen zuerst immer alleine! Einerseits, um Abschied zu nehmen, andererseits – und das ist wohl das Wichtigste –, um selbstkritisch die Grundrisse zu prüfen.

CW   Wir haben bis jetzt nur über Grundrisse gesprochen. Wohnungen können aber auch mehrgeschossig sein, und damit rückt der Schnitt, die Vertikale, in den Vordergrund. Wie geht ihr damit um?

LS   Ein gutes Beispiel dafür ist das bereits erwähnte Wohnhaus an der Meret Oppenheim-Strasse. Das ist unser Versuch, jedem Raum auch in der dritten Dimension Bedeutung zu geben. Wir möchten unterschiedliche Raumerlebnisse inszenieren. Im Studium an

PG   What you're talking about is the individual autobiography of dwelling. This can also be formulated in another way: it's about what a person knows best and what's most familiar. For example, I'd like to build airports, but I can't really apply my experience to something like this. It's different with dwelling. Dwelling, my own experience of dwelling, has always interested me. I grew up in a duplex that my father built in the spirit of Le Corbusier—everything in exposed concrete. When I started going to school and invited friends home, they said, "Poor you! You're still-ing living on a construction site." That bothered me a lot. I think that's one of the reasons why I'm still so preoccupied with dwelling today—where do I feel comfortable, how do I create coziness, and so on. That's also my response to your original question about how we approach things. This is something that Luca and I unconsciously have in common: we keep referring back again and again to our own experience. Christoph, you mentioned calibration and how to get from there to a quality of scale. I've noticed that some architects no longer have any idea how big a table or how high a kitchen shelf ought to be. They lack the ability to relate to dimensions. Maybe this has to do with drawing with computers. We're privileged in that we've been able to work hard to acquire this experience. Maybe that's a little bit of the secret of our success. You mentioned the diagonal and other similar aspects; to have a knack for this, first of all the proper basis is needed. When I follow your work, Luca, I sense how this experience, this richness, is injected. And that's always the good thing about having personally executed projects: after completing an apartment building, I always visit it the first time alone! On the one hand, to say goodbye, and on the other—and that is probably the main reason—to self-critically check the floor plans.

CW   So far we've only talked about floor plans. However, apartments can also be multistory, meaning that the section, the vertical, becomes the

der ETH Zürich hat uns Dolf Schnebli immer gesagt: «Entwerft zweigeschossige Wohnungen!» Aber da fehlt der Zwischenton. Der eine Tritt, den es hinauf- oder hinuntergeht, das ist die reiche Welt, die ich meine. Im Studium wollten wir herausfinden, wie Adolf Loos das gemacht hat. Es gab Modelle seiner Bauten, aus denen wir gelernt haben, dass er die komplizierten Stellen einfach als Hohlräume beliess.

PG Wir müssen auch wieder lernen, mit Leerräumen umzugehen. Wir verbinden den Raum immer mit dem Licht, mit der Lichtführung. Man könnte auch einmal zweigeschossige Räume entwerfen, in denen man wenig Licht hat, wie wir das beim Hochhaus Hard Turm Park in Zürich [Wettbewerb: 2007; Planung und Ausführung: 2010–2013] gemacht haben. Man könnte sie gleich noch schwarz anmalen. Denn man kann die dritte Dimension auch ohne Licht erkunden. Wenn man in sechs oder sieben Schichten baut, ergibt sich vielleicht plötzlich das Potenzial, dass man innen liegende Räume schaffen und schön ausleuchten kann. Im Museum finden wir das toll, wir gehen von Raum zu Raum und vom Tageslicht ist keine Spur. Dafür etwas Mut zu haben, finde ich wichtig.

LS Es gibt solche Orte, an denen man 25–30 Meter Raumtiefe inszenieren und erleben kann. Es braucht einfach einen Bauherrn mit gleicher Neugierde. Ich bin überzeugt, dass daraus würdige Räume entstehen können — und damit würdige Architektur. Der Begriff der Würde beschäftigt uns je länger, je mehr. Wie bauen wir würdige Häuser? Das macht sich zum Beispiel am Material fest. Wie willst du Würde mit verputztem Styropor erzeugen? Unser Büro liegt im Gebäudekomplex der Markthalle Basel, die ist über 90 Jahre alt. Da wurde die Klinkerfassade im Sockel noch nie neu gemacht und man spürt die Würde dieses Gebäudes mit den Originalmaterialien. Klar, das ist romantisch, aber ich glaube auch, dass die Häuser eine Seele entwickeln, die sich mit dem Leben der Menschen verbinden lässt.

major emphasis. How do you deal with this aspect?

LS A good example of this is the residential building on Meret Oppenheim-Strasse I mentioned before. This is our attempt to give every space significance, including in the third dimension. We want to stage different spatial experiences. During my studies in architecture at ETH Zurich, Dolf Schnebli always told us, "Design two-story apartments!" But here the subtext is missing. What I mean by richness is the difference in level, up or down, by one single step. During our studies we wanted to find out how Adolf Loos did it. There were models of his buildings from which we learned that he simply left the complicated spots as hollow spaces.

PG We also had to relearn how to deal with empty spaces. We always connect a room with lighting, with directing daylight. Once in a while we've managed to design two-story spaces in which there is little light, as we did for Hard Turm Park Tower in Zurich [Competition: 2007; Planning and Execution: 2010–2013]. Because the third dimension can also be explored without light, theoretically it's possible to just paint them black. When you build in six or seven layers, maybe a potential suddenly emerges for creating internally located spaces and illuminating them nicely. For us, that's the great thing in a museum: you walk from space to space and there's no trace of daylight. I think it's important to be brave enough to try this.

LS There are some places where spatial depths of 25 to 30 meters can be staged and experienced. All it needs is a client who has the same degree of curiosity. I'm convinced situations like this can generate dignified spaces—and with them dignified architecture. The longer we've worked with the concept of dignifying, the more it engages us. How do we build dignified houses? This is firmly connected, for instance, with the material. How can you expect to create dignity with plastered styrofoam? Our office is located in the Markthalle Basel complex, which is over ninety years old. The clinker façade of the

Adolf Loos hat das Prinzip des Kammergrundrisses in die dritte Dimension übertragen. Der Raumplan umfasst, wie hier bei der Villa Müller in Prag (1930), je nach funktionalen Anforderungen aber auch Korridore.

The principle of the chambered floor plan translated into the third dimension. As demonstrated here in the Villa Müller (1930), Prague, by Adolf Loos, depending on functional requirements the spatial plan can also include corridors.

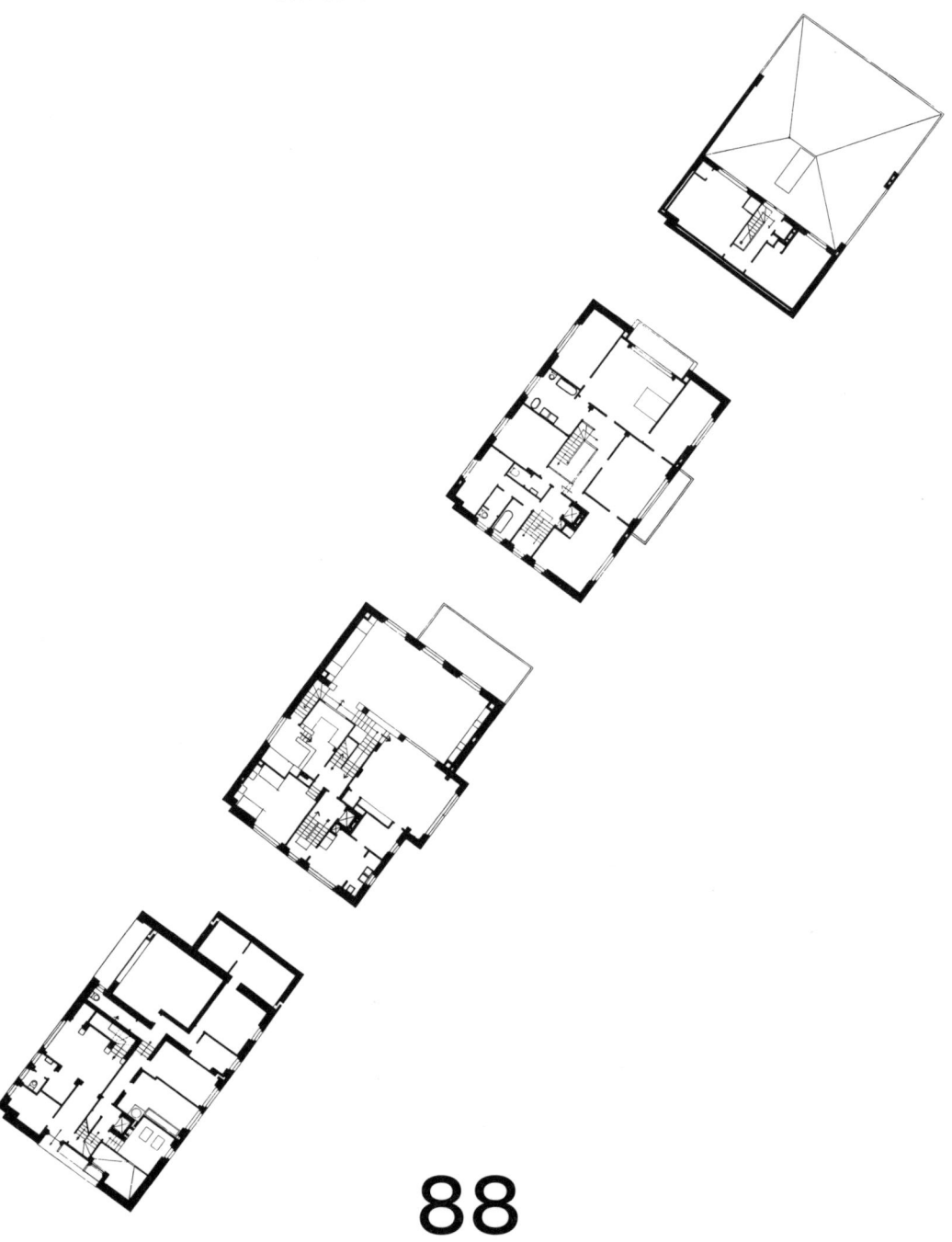

CW Du hast von der Neugier gesprochen, die euch antreibt. Aber braucht es nicht auch die Neugier der Bewohnerinnen und Bewohner? Wie ist es um deren Neugier bestellt?

LS Ich bin der Meinung, wenn sich ein Grundriss mit dem Leben nicht richtig verbinden lässt, ist er gescheitert. Man sollte den Nutzern nicht erklären müssen, wie sie die Wohnung zu gebrauchen haben. Das alles hat mit Sorgfalt, Respekt und Liebe zu tun. Du spürst einfach, mit welcher Haltung jemand das entworfen hat, und das wird sich in den Räumen manifestieren.

PG Vermutlich sind nicht die Neugier, sondern die alltäglichen Bedürfnisse entscheidend. Die Nutzer der Wohnungen sind ja nicht dumm. Sie merken sofort, was praktisch ist und was nicht, ob ein Grundriss tauglich ist oder nicht. Das schönste Lob, das ich bekommen habe von einer Mieterin, ist: Ich will da nie mehr raus. Das finde ich toll, sie schätzt die Möglichkeiten, die ihr die Wohnung gibt. Bei der Kammerung stellt sich zum Beispiel die Frage der Zirkulation. Hat ein Raum mehrere Türen, entstehen zusätzliche Verbindungen, die den Raum grösser machen. Das sind Eigenschaften und Qualitäten, die die Leute bemerken.

CW Das Thema der Erschliessung ist zentral, bietet die Kammerung doch die Möglichkeit, auf Erschliessungsräume zu verzichten. Damit ist der Kammergrundriss das Gegenteil eines Korridortyps. Und trotzdem braucht es natürlich eine Erschliessung und die Möglichkeit zur Zirkulation. Wenn ich zum Beispiel eure Wohnhäuser für Studierende und das Personal des Universitätsspitals in Zürich anschaue, Patrick, dann sind die Zimmer zwar klassische Kammern. Aber die Erschliessungsfigur ist aus dieser Kammerung herausgenommen und bildet ein Leitmotiv des Entwurfs. Beim Erlenmatt-Schulhaus [Neubau Primarschule Erlenmatt, Basel, Wettbewerb: 2012; Planung und Ausführung: 2013–2017 → 23] von Luca Selva Architekten sind die Schulzimmer als Kammern ausgebildet. Der öffentliche Raum mit pedestal has never been redone and the dignified quality of this building can be sensed through the original material. Sure, that's romantic, but I also believe that buildings develop a soul that can connect with people's lives.

CW You mentioned the curiosity that drives you. But isn't the curiosity of the inhabitants equally important? What about their curiosity?

LS My opinion is that if a floor plan doesn't connect properly with the way people live in a place, it's failed. It shouldn't be necessary to explain to occupants how they have to use the apartment. Everything has to do with care, respect, and love. You just sense the stance someone took in designing it and this approach will be manifest in the spaces.

PG It's probably not curiosity but everyday needs that are decisive. The users of the apartments are not exactly dumb. They notice right away what's practical and what's not; whether a floor plan is suitable or not. The best praise I ever received from a tenant is, "I never want to move out." I think that's great—she appreciates the possibilities that the apartment gives to her. In the case of chambering, one question that occurs, as an example, is circulation. If a space has several doors, additional connections are created that make the space larger. These are traits and qualities that people notice.

CW Circulation is the crux, and in fact chambering offers the opportunity to dispense with circulation spaces. In this respect the chambered floor plan is the opposite of a corridor type. Nevertheless, of course, access is necessary, and the possibility to circulate. Patrick, when I look, for instance, at your residential buildings for the students and staff of the University Hospital in Zurich, the rooms are evidently classic chambers but the circulation figure has been separated from this chambering and forms a distinct design leitmotif. At the Erlenmatt Primary Schoolhouse [New Erlenmatt Primary School, Basel. Competition: 2012; Planning and Execution: 2013–2017 → 23] by

den Treppen schraubt sich relativ frei durch das Gebäude, folgt aber immer noch der Logik der Kammerung. Wie ist das Verhältnis von Erschliessung und Kammerung?

LS   Es braucht immer einen Ort, um die Schuhe und den Mantel auszuziehen. Deshalb gibt es immer dort, wo man eintritt, Sondersituationen. Die Idee ist, das so unhierarchisch wie möglich anzulegen. Für uns ist alles wichtig, also auch das Hineinkommen. Im Kaltbrunnen-Schulhaus gibt es eine Erschliessungshalle, die doppelt so gross ist wie ein Klassenzimmer. Das Unhierarchische zeigt sich hier auch an den Materialien, es sind überall die gleichen Platten verlegt — an den Arbeitsplätzen wie in den WCs →12. Das ist etwas, das uns grundsätzlich interessiert.

PG   Wir schauen insbesondere auf die Zirkulation. Die Zirkulation innerhalb der Wohnung ist ein Mittel, um die Wohnung grösser zu machen, etwa wenn ich von einem Raum zum anderen verschiedene Wege gehen kann. Die Erschliessung ist ein Element, das den Unterschied ausmachen kann. Mit den Treppen oder mit der Belichtung kann Reichtum erzeugt werden. Wir haben in den 1990er-Jahren eine gute Erfahrung gemacht: Damals haben wir noch nichts gebaut, konnten aber eine Wohnung kaufen und hatten dort das erste Mal Gelegenheit, die eigene Wohnform zu erkunden. Wie will ich wohnen? Es war ein Haus von Gret Loewensberg an der Hinterbergstrasse in Zürich [1997–1999], dort hatten wir die Attikawohnung, die schön, aber auch knapp bemessen war. Wir haben lange über diesem Grundriss gebrütet und schliesslich den Gang weggelassen. Wir haben ein Entree gemacht, von dem aus man direkt in die Küche und ins Wohnzimmer oder eben in die Garderobe und ins Tages-WC mit zwei Türen oder ins Bad gehen konnte. Das war eine wichtige Erfahrung, all diese Räume zu machen, die dann jeweils ein, zwei oder drei Türen hatten, die verschiedene Bewegungen ermöglichten. Das Öffnen und Schliessen von Türen ist hochinteressant. Man hat einen

Luca Selva Architekten, the classrooms are designed as chambered units. The shared space with the stairway twists relatively freely through the building but still follows the logic of chambering. What is the relationship between circulation and chambering?

LS   A place to take off your shoes and coat is always needed. That's why the point where you enter is always a special situation. The idea is to lay this out as non-hierarchically as possible. For us, everything is important, including how you come in. In the Kaltbrunnen Schoolhouse there's a circulation hall that's twice the size of a classroom. The non-hierarchical is also evident here in the materials: the same floor tiles have been laid everywhere—in the workplaces as well as in the WCs →12. This is something that we're fundamentally interested in.

PG   We pay special attention to the circulation. The circulation within an apartment is a means of making the apartment larger; for example, if I can take different routes to go from one space to another. Circulation is an element that can make all the difference. Richness can be created with the stairs or by directing daylight. We had some good training in this in the 1990s. At that time we hadn't built anything yet, but we were able to buy an apartment and there we had the first opportunity to explore our own form of dwelling. How do I want to live? The building was by Gret Loewensberg on Hinterbergstrasse in Zurich, built between 1997 and 1999, where we had the roof apartment, which was beautiful but also slightly a squeeze. We struggled a lot with this floor plan and finally omitted the corridor. We made an entrance hall from where you could go directly into the kitchen and into the living room, or even into the cloakroom and into the separate WC with two doors, or into the bathroom. Creating all these spaces was an important experience, as each of them had one, two, or three doors that allow you to take a different route. Opening and closing doors is extremely interesting. Having

Raum, kann den zweiten und dritten noch anschliessen und hat damit eine Enfilade. Mit verschiedenen Oberflächen, Bodenbelägen und Farben kann man den Räumen eigene Stimmungen geben. Das ist die Chance, die die Zirkulation eröffnet. Wenn das dann noch kombiniert ist mit undefinierten Räumen, wird es interessant. Wir sollten davon abkommen festzulegen, wo man schläft, isst und so weiter. Wo früher das Sofa stand, steht jetzt das Rennvelo.

CW Wenn eine Wohnung Freiheiten bietet, ist das eine grosse Qualität. Luca, du hast davon gesprochen, dass ihr einmal zwei einspännig erschlossene Baumgartner-Wohnungen vertikal verbunden habt, was natürlich nochmals eine neue Dimension eröffnet. Wie bist du dabei vorgegangen?

LS Die erwähnte Koppelung hat mich etwa anderthalb Jahre lang beschäftigt. Wir haben schliesslich nur einen Deckenbalken herausgenommen und dazwischen eine sehr steile Treppe angeordnet. Man glaubt kaum, was dann plötzlich räumlich passiert! Es war Denksport mit unglaublich befriedigendem Ausgang. Im oberen Geschoss war jede Wand ein wenig verrückt, was wir erst jetzt wahrgenommen haben. So ein Baumgartner-Haus ist ja quasi ein Archetyp, sehr präzise gefügt.

PG Zwei Wohnungen zusammenzuführen, ist sind eine Herausforderung! Plötzlich hast du zwei Küchen. Was macht man mit zwei Wohnzimmern? Eine Erfahrung, die ich gemacht habe, ist der Ansatz, Wohnen und Essen möglichst weit auseinanderzunehmen. Das ergibt auf den ersten Blick vielleicht keinen Sinn, bewirkt aber, dass man die ganze Wohnung nutzt. Wir haben das an der Hinterbergstrasse gemacht, Küche und Essen da, Wohnen auf der anderen Seite. Das brachte viel Bewegung in die Räume. Wenn ich schon viel Platz habe, wie kann ich die Räume täglich nutzen? Seit wir keinen Fernseher mehr haben, brauchen wir das Wohnzimmer nicht mehr. Da sind wir wieder bei den Nutzungen. Das Wohnen geht über den Grundriss hinaus. Der Grundriss ist nur die Hülle.

one space, the second and third can be conjoined and the result is an enfilade. Through different surface treatments, flooring, and color schemes, the spaces can be given their own moods. That's the scope that circulation gives you. And when this opportunity is combined with undefined spaces, things get interesting. We ought to stop telling people they should sleep here, eat there, and so on. Nowadays, the niche where the sofa used to sit is where the racing bike gets parked!

CW It really enhances the quality when an apartment offers freedom. Luca, you mentioned that you once connected two Baumgartner apartments vertically that were originally only accessible via individual entries— an intervention which naturally opens up a new dimension. How did you go about doing this?

LS The coupling mentioned earlier kept me busy for about one and a half years. In the end we only removed a single ceiling beam and inserted a very steep staircase in between. It's almost unbelievable what suddenly happened then spatially! It was a brainteaser with an incredibly satisfying outcome. On the upper floor every wall was a bit crazy, which we've only just realized now. A Baumgartner house like this is in fact a quasi archetype, put together very precisely.

PG Combining two apartments into one is challenging! All of a sudden you have two kitchens. What do you do with two living rooms? An approach I've learned is to separate the living and dining areas as much as possible. At first, this might not seem to make any sense, but the effect is that you use the entire apartment. We did this with Hinterbergstrasse: kitchen and dining here, living and sleeping spaces on the other side over there. That brought a lot of movement into the spaces. If I already have a lot of room, how can I use the spaces on a daily basis? Since we no longer have a television, we don't need a living room anymore. Here we come back to usage again. Dwelling transcends the floor plan. The floor plan is just the shell.

LS   Auch hier gilt, er muss Würde ausstrahlen. Ich habe vor Kurzem in einem Interview mit Aki Kaurismäki gelesen, er arbeite mit Würde, nicht mit Make-up. Es gibt ja fast keine würdigeren Menschen als jene in Kaurismäkis Filmen. Wir produzieren so viel Architektur, die auf dem «Prinzip Make-up» basiert. Es wird schöngeschminkt für den Moment. Das hat auch etwas mit dem Vertrieb zu tun: Eine Eigentumswohnung muss einmal schön sein, nämlich bis du dich zum Kauf entschlossen hast. Sieht man sich etwa die Mietskasernen in Berlin-Kreuzberg an, mit ihren zweiten und dritten Hinterhöfen, dann ist das beengt und doch spürt man immer die Würde, denn die Dinge wollen nicht mehr sein, als sie sind. Und man versteht, was Alvaro Siza 1986 zur IBA Berlin motiviert hat, in einer unfassbaren architektonischen Sinnlichkeit zu intervenieren. Was heisst heute Architektur und Würde? In der Gründerzeit ist es gelungen, Stadtmuster zu entwickeln, die heute noch Bestand haben. Haben wir das auch geschafft? Die Architekturhistorikerin Dorothee Huber sagte immer, in ihren *Architekturführer Basel* nehme sie ungern Bauten auf, die jünger als 25 Jahre sind, weil sie einfach noch nicht weiss, ob sie halten oder nicht. Es braucht diese Generation, die darübergeht, um die Gültigkeit zu beweisen. Wenn ich in Basel die Latte ganz hoch lege, dann muss ich sagen: Die Warteck-Überbauung von Roger Diener wird jeden Tag besser. Die Häuser an der Hammerstrasse werden jetzt äusserlich verunstaltet, aber räumlich funktionieren sie immer noch. Und was wird aus unseren Siedlungen? Werden die Bauten des Densa-Areals in 20 Jahren eine Referenz sein? Ich hoffe es, aber es wird sich erst zeigen müssen.

PG   Wir leben in einer spannenden Zeit, weil wir viel Arbeit haben. Aber gleichzeitig haben wir ein Problem, weil der Wert unserer Arbeit nicht mehr anerkannt wird. Hier wieder das richtige Mass zu finden, wäre ganz wichtig. Man flieht mitunter in die Grundrissakrobatik, weil so viele andere Parameter schon

LS   What also holds true in this case is that the ground plan has to radiate a dignity. Recently I read an interview with Aki Kaurismäki in which he said that he works with dignity, not makeup. There are hardly any figures more ennobled than those in Kaurismäki's films. We produce so much architecture based on the "makeup principle." Everything's prettified for the moment. This also has something to do with marketing. A condominium has to be beautiful only once, namely until the customer's decided to buy it. If you look at the workers tenement blocks in Berlin-Kreuzberg, with their second- and third-tier rear courtyards, although conditions are cramped you still sense a certain dignity, simply because the things don't want to be more than what they are. And it's understandable what drove Alvaro Siza when he took part in the IBA Berlin in 1986 to intervene with such an incredible architectural sensuality. What does architecture and dignity mean today? In the German-Austrian Gründerzeit they managed to develop cityscapes with a substance that still today has a vital built relevance. Have we achieved the same? Historian of architecture Dorothee Huber always says that she's reluctant to include buildings less than twenty-five years old in her architecture guidebook to Basel because she simply doesn't know whether they'll last or not. A generation has to pass in order for their validity to be proven. If I was asked to say what I think the gold standard is, in Basel I'd simply say that Roger Diener's Warteckof project gets better and better every day. The exterior of the apartment buildings on Hammerstrasse has been mutilated, but they still function spatially. And what will become of our apartment projects? Will the buildings on the Densa-Areal be a reference in twenty years? I hope so, but it remains to be seen.

PG   We're personally experiencing an exciting phase because we have a lot of work to do. But likewise we're faced with a problem because the value of our work is no longer acknowledged. Finding the right balance would be very

vorbestimmt sind. Ich war neulich in einer Jury und habe einen neuen Begriff gelernt, der mich anschliessend sehr beschäftigt hat: der Begriff der Loser-Wohnung. Wie viele Loser-Wohnungen gibt es? «Ah, das Projekt hat keine, das nehmen wir», sagten die Investoren. Die Grundrisse waren grauenvoll, aber keiner war schlecht belichtet. Wie bewegen wir uns in diesem Umfeld? Du hast von Würde gesprochen, Luca. Die muss man in den Jurys wieder einmal einbringen. Vielleicht braucht es da wieder mehr Rückgrat, damit man auch mal als Juror sagen kann: «Das geht nicht.» Für guten Städtebau und gute Architektur müssen wir wieder lernen, all diese Dinge, die wir besprechen, auch nach aussen zu tragen. Nur so entfalten sie eine weitergehende Wirkung.

important. Sometimes the acrobatics of the floor plan become a refuge, because so many other parameters have already been predetermined. Recently, serving on a jury, I learned the new term "loser apartment" that I couldn't stop thinking about afterwards. "How many loser apartments are there? Okay, that project doesn't have any? We'll take it," said the investors. The floor plans were horrific, but none of them were poorly daylit. If that's the context, where exactly are we heading? You spoke of dignity, Luca. Juries have to be rewired in this respect. Maybe more resolve is required again so that also as a juror you can say, "enough is enough." Good urban planning and good architecture require us to learn to communicate all the things we've discussed right here to the outside world again. That's the only way things can take on a deeper resonance.

Der modulare Grundriss des Einfamilienhauses Sunnebüel verbindet in der Vertikalen und Horizontalen die Kammern zu grosszügigen Raumfolgen. Mit Schiebe- und Klappelementen können die räumlichen Zuordnungen verändert werden. Eigenheim der Architektin Lux Guyer in Küsnacht, 1930.

> Architect Lux Guyer's home, Küsnacht (1930). The modular floor plan of the single-family Sunnebüel house connects the chambers vertically and horizontally in generous spatial sequences. The spatial configurations can be changed via sliding elements.
>
> ↓

Auch hier soll für ein ehemaliges Industriegelände eine städtebauliche Strategie entstehen. In der frei platzierten Häusergruppe, die insgesamt 100 Wohnungen aufnimmt, werden drei, vier oder fünf parallel gekammerte Schichten gesetzt. Dieses Schichtensystem bildet in der Längsrichtung eine klar ablesbare Morphologie und schafft im Grundriss hallenartige, gut proportionierte Räume mit grosszügiger Belichtung.

> Here, too, an urban development strategy is to be applied for reusing a former industrial site. In the freely placed group of residential buildings, which accommodate a total of one hundred apartments, three, four, or five parallel chambered layers are employed. This layered system forms a clearly legible morphology in the longitudinal direction and creates layouts with hall-like, well-proportioned spaces with generous daylight exposure. Giessereiareal housing development, Liestal, invited study commission, Giesserei Erzenberg AG: 2018.
>
> → →

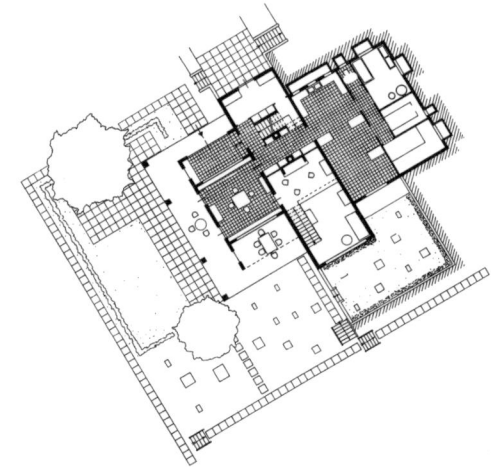

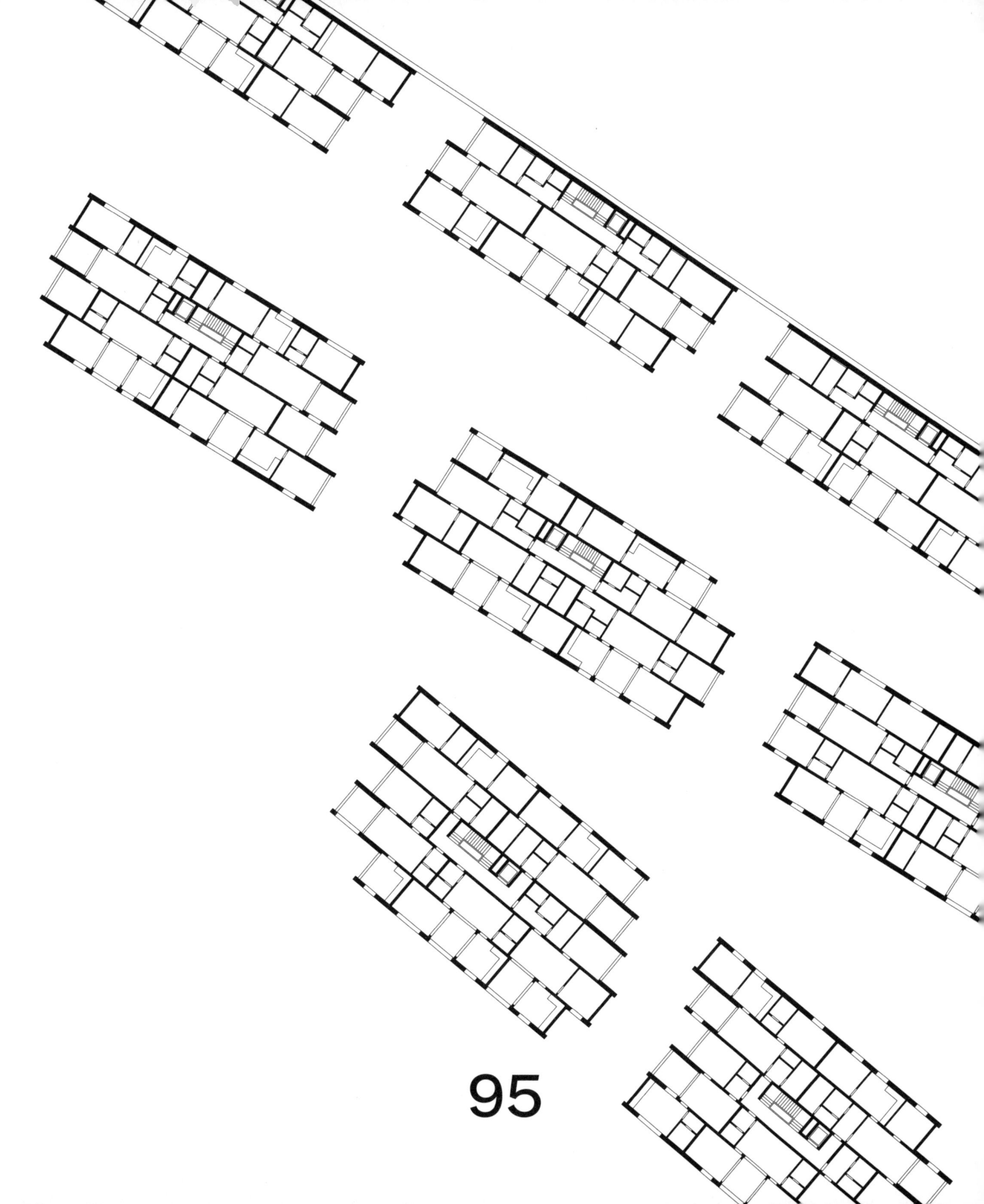

Ausgebildet als funktionales Hofhaus, zeigen sich in diesem Projekt die Eigenheiten eines für die mediterrane Klimazone geplanten Bauwerks. Die unter freiem Himmel liegenden Aussenräume sind in den weitgehend geschlossenen Grundriss eingebunden. Das Erdgeschoss nimmt die repräsentativen Räume und Büros auf, während sich die privaten Räume des Botschafters im ersten Obergeschoss befinden. Neubau der Wohnresidenz des Schweizer Botschafters in Algier, Algerien, Wettbewerb im selektiven Verfahren: 2017.

    Articulated as a functional courtyard building, this project demonstrates typical features of structures designed for a Mediterranean climate. The open-air exterior areas are integrated into the largely closed floor plan. The ground floor houses the representative spaces and offices, while the ambassador's private quarters are located on the upper first floor. New residence of the Swiss Ambassador in Algiers, Algeria, selective competition entry: 2017.

↓

Das unhierarchische Prinzip des Kammergrundrisses wurde im Orient auf ganze Städte übertragen. Mauer an Mauer stehen die Häuser, deren Höfe durch innere Verdichtung immer kleiner wurden. Quartier Banqusa im Nordosten der Altstadt von Aleppo (Syrien).

    Banqusa neighborhood in the northeastern area of the historic center of Aleppo (Syria). In some ancient Near East settlements, the non-hierarchical principle of the chambered floor plan was applied to the entire urban fabric. The houses stand wall-to-wall, the inner densification making the courtyards smaller and smaller.

→

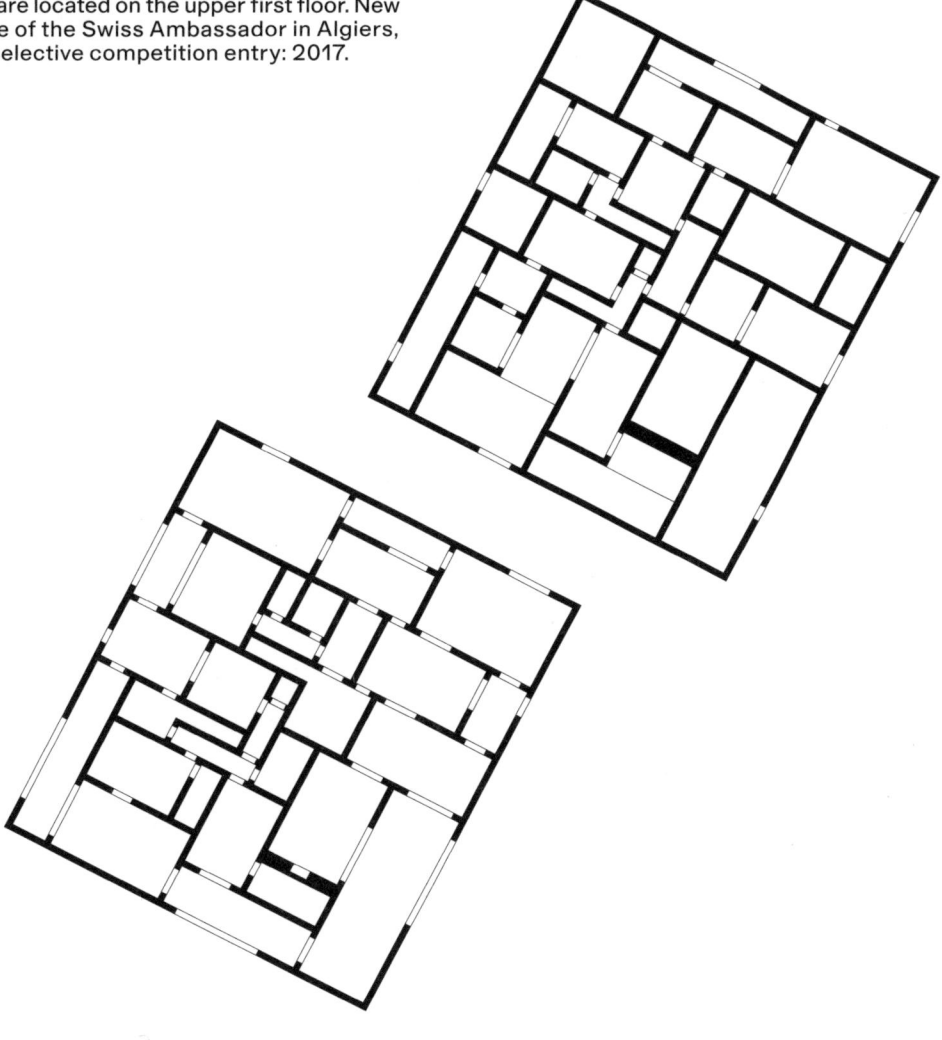

97

Wie bei einem Puzzle greifen die einzelnen Höfe und Kammern ineinander als Abbild der Familien- und Besitzergeschichte. Bei diesem Haus in Aleppo wurde der Durchgang (B) geschlossen, wodurch zwei Einheiten entstanden.

At this house in Aleppo, two units were created by closing a passageway (B). Like a puzzle, the individual courtyards and chambers interlock, reflecting the history of the families and owners.

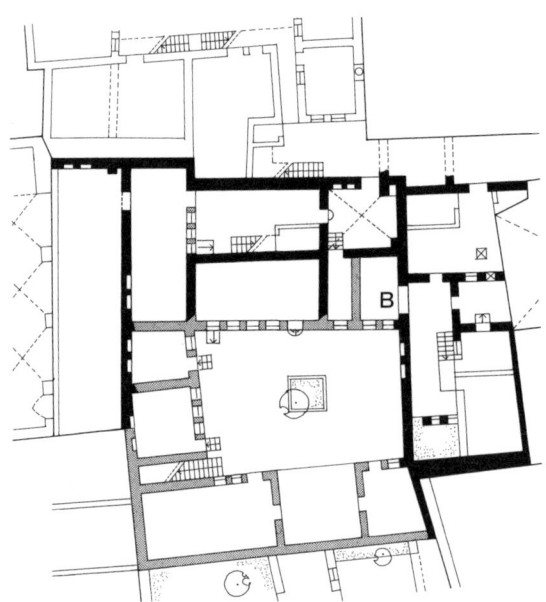

Ein geschlossenes äusseres Volumen und räumlich ineinandergreifende Strukturen im Innern, Räume verschiedener Dimensionen und eine komplexe, dabei aber strenge Ordnung des Grundrisses charakterisieren dieses Dienstleistungszentrum. Innen und aussen liegende Lichthöfe eröffnen überraschende Blickbeziehungen. Neubau Gemeindezentrum Pratteln, Projektwettbewerb, Gemeinde Pratteln: 2018.

The community service center is characterized by a closed external volume and spatially interlocking structures in the interior, spaces with various dimensions, and a complex but nonetheless strict arrangement of the floor plan. Inner and outer atriums open up surprising visual connections. New Pratteln Community Center, competition project, Municipality of Pratteln: 2018.

↓

Auch im ländlichen Raum gibt es Siedlungen, die fast ausschliesslich aus Häusern mit Kammergrundrissen bestehen. In Soglio (Graubünden) weisen die Holz- und Steinbauten nahezu dieselbe Maschenweite auf, sodass ein einheitliches Bild entsteht.

Chambered settlement structure, Soglio (Graubünden). Settlements consisting almost exclusively of houses with chambered floor plans also exist in rural areas. In Soglio the wooden and stone buildings display nearly the same mesh size, creating a cohesive settlement fabric.

→

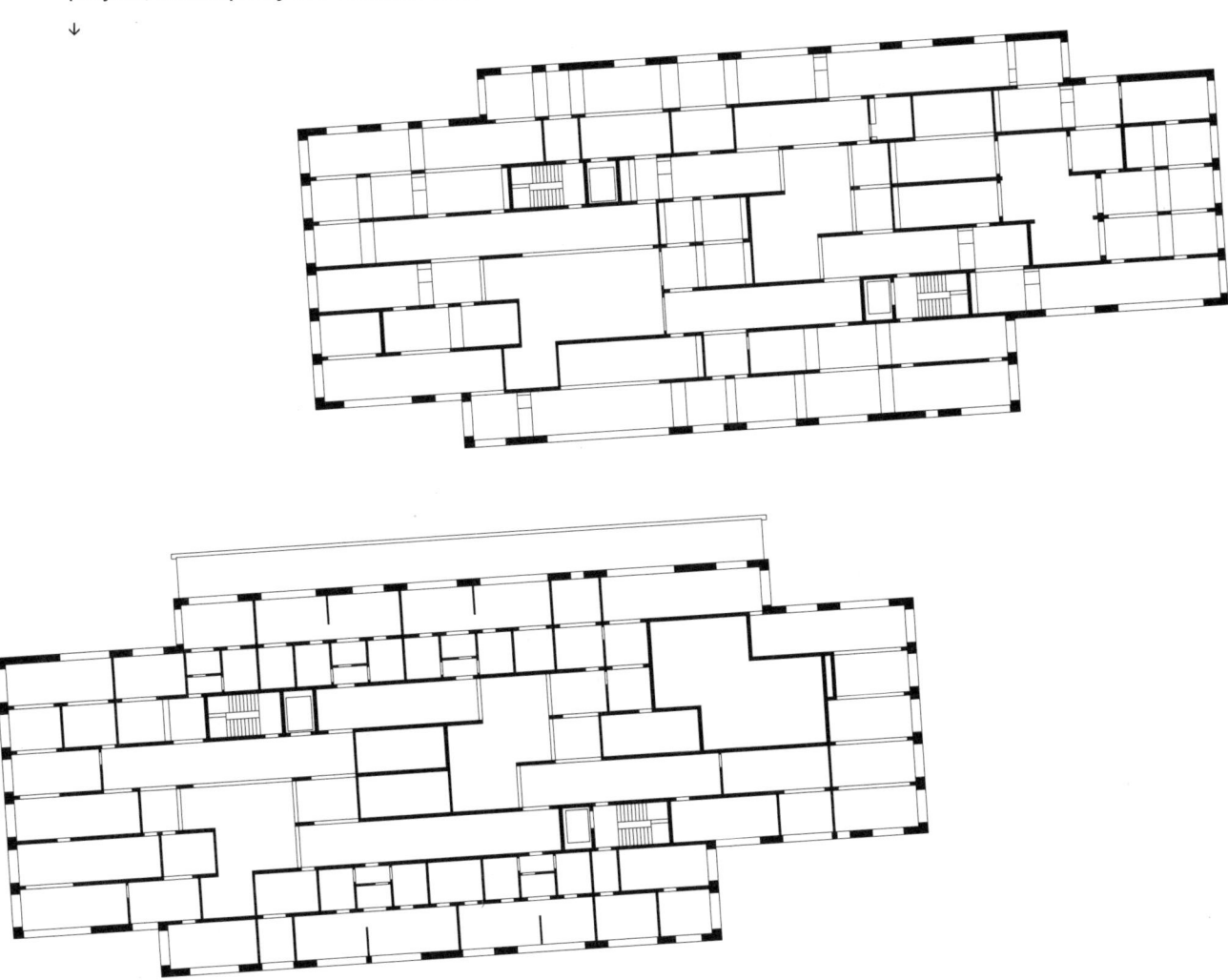

Wunsch der Auftraggeberin waren zwei voneinander unabhängige Wohneinheiten in einem Gebäude. Dabei ist nicht nur ein von unterschiedlich grossen Räumen geprägter Grundriss entstanden, sondern eine virtuose dreidimensionale Verschachtelung verschieden hoher Strukturen. Mehrgenerationenwohnhaus, Binningen, Privatauftrag, Projekt: 2010; Fertigstellung: 2013.

The client's specifications entailed incorporating two independent residential units in one building. The result is not only a floor plan characterized by various space sizes but also a skillful three-dimensional interlacing of structures with different heights. Multi-generational residential building, Binningen, private commission, project: 2010; completion: 2013.

← ↓ →

Die Komplexität des Mehrgenerationenhauses erschliesst sich im Plan, noch besser aber beim Blick auf die isometrischen Darstellungen.

The complexity of the multi-generational residential building is evident in the plan, but is even more apparent in the isometric drawings.

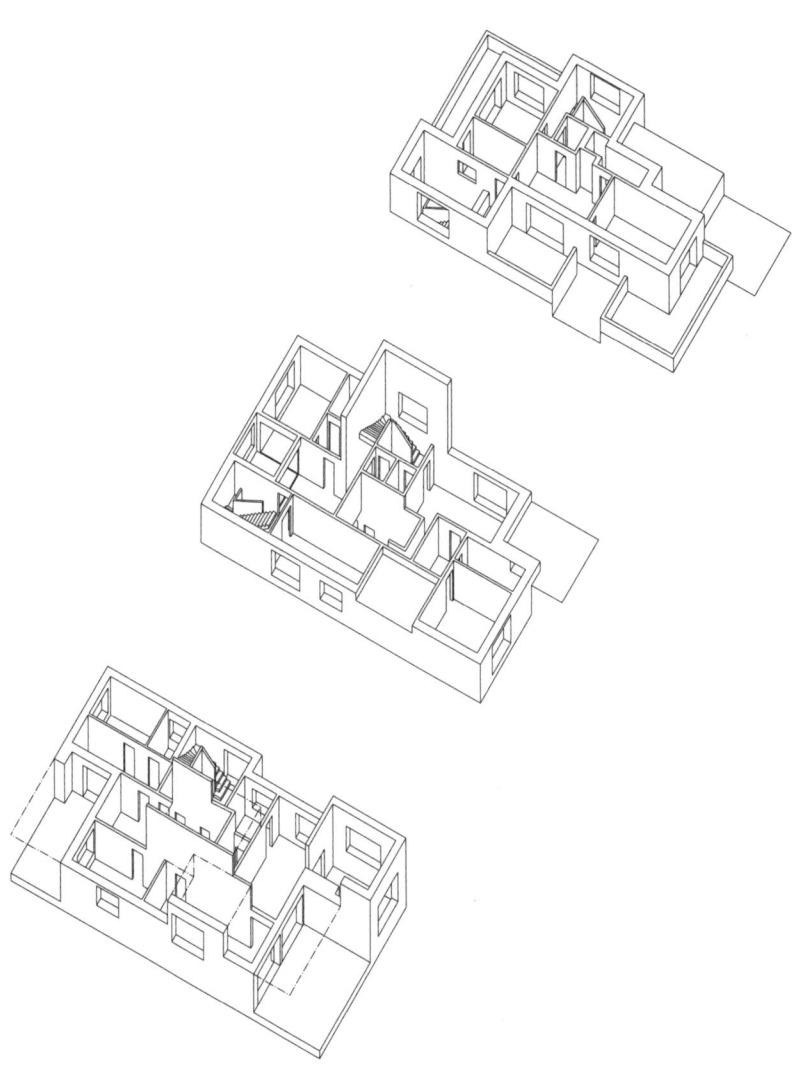

Biografien
Biographies

Luca Selva Architekten

1991 in Basel gegründet, wird das Büro von Luca Selva mit Roger Braccini, Sonja Christen und David Gschwind geführt. Ihre Suche nach dem Wesentlichen einer jeden Bauaufgabe mündet in ein architektonisches Leitmotiv, das zu einer passgenauen Lösung verdichtet wird. Diese überzeugt langfristig durch ihre Selbstverständlichkeit und Effizienz und trägt den materiellen wie immateriellen Werten gleichermassen Rechnung. Das Büro bearbeitet das ganze Spektrum vom Entwurf über die Konstruktion und Materialwahl bis zur Realisierung. Schwerpunkte seiner Tätigkeit bilden der Wohnungsbau, städtebauliche Studien sowie öffentliche Bauten und Umbauten.

1996 gelang mit dem Kaltbrunnen-Schulhaus in Basel (mit Jean Pierre Wymann) der Durchbruch. Ebenfalls in Basel steht das Primarschulhaus Erlenmatt (2017), das die Recherche zum Schulbau weiterführt. Internationale Beachtung fand – neben dem Ordos-Projekt mit Ai Weiwei (2008) – der Nachwuchs-Campus des FC Basel (2013). Das Doppelwohnhaus Bäumlihof in Riehen (2001) und das preisgekrönte Mehrgenerationenhaus in Binningen (2013) stehen für Einfamilienhäuser mit besonderem Raumprogramm. Die Wohnsiedlung Densa-Areal in Basel (2012) und die Genossenschaftswohnungen Linth-Escher in Zürich-Oerlikon (2012) markieren Eckpunkte in der Entwicklung grösserer Wohnbauprojekte, die derzeit mit der Planung in einem denkmalgeschützten Industriekontext in Köln (2015–2022) und mit dem Furnierwerk-Areal in Rheinfelden (2012–2020) fortgesetzt wird.

Zwei Bücher widmen sich der Arbeit von Luca Selva Architekten; sie wurde mit zahlreichen Preisen und Auszeichnungen bedacht und wird breit publiziert. Dazu kommt eine rege Ausstellungstätigkeit: 2012 und 2014 war das Büro an der Architekturbiennale in Venedig präsent, und die Architektur Galerie Berlin zeigte unter dem Titel *Acht Fenster* eine thematische Installation. Das Büro ist in der Basler Markthalle domiziliert und beschäftigt derzeit rund 30 Mitarbeitende.

was founded in Basel in 1991 and is directed by Luca Selva with Roger Braccini, Sonja Christen, and David Gschwind. Seeking the essentials of every building task leads to an architectural leitmotif that is then condensed into a tailor-made solution. Over the long term, this approach has proven to be convincing on account of its matter-of-fact simplicity and efficiency while equally addressing material as well as immaterial values. The firm's range of work spans an entire spectrum of services from preliminary design to construction, and on to the choice of materials and execution. Specialties encompass housing, urban studies, public buildings, and reuse/renovations.

The Kaltbrunnen Schoolhouse (1996) in Basel (realized with Jean-Pierre Wymann) marked an initial breakthrough into the field. Also in Basel, the Erlenmatt Primary Schoolhouse (2017) represents a continuation of research concerning school buildings. The FC Basel Youngster Campus (2013), along with participation in 2008 in the Ordos 100 project with Ai Weiwei, brought the firm international recognition. The Bäumlihof Duplex (2001) in Riehen and the award-winning Multigenerational House (2013) in Binningen represent single-family homes with special spatial programming. The Densa Park Residential Complex (2012) in Basel and the Linth-Escher Cooperative Apartments (2012) in Zurich-Oerlikon are milestones in the development of larger housing projects. This experience is currently being advanced in the context of a project (2015–2022) within an industrial historic landmark area in Cologne (Germany) and in the Furnierwerk Residential Project (2012–2020) at the site of a former veneer factory in Rheinfelden.

Luca Selva Architekten's works have been acknowledged through numerous prizes and awards and have been extensively written about, including two books devoted solely to them. This widespread reputation is underscored by ongoing engagement in exhibitions: in 2012 and 2014 the firm was shown at the Venice Biennale of Architecture, and in 2015 the Architektur Galerie Berlin presented a thematic installation entitled *Eight Windows*. Currently employing around thirty people, the office of Luca Selva Architekten is located at the Markthalle Basel.

Patrick Gmür ist Architekt ETH/BSA/SIA und Stadtplaner, Mitinhaber des Architekturbüros Steib Gmür Geschwentner Kyburz Partner AG in Zürich und seit 2016 Vorsitzender des Gestaltungsbeirats in Stuttgart. Er juriert zudem als Experte in Architektur und Stadtplanung regelmässig Wettbewerbe im In- und Ausland. Daneben hatte er verschiedene Professuren beziehungsweise Gastprofessuren inne, beispielsweise an der FHNW in Basel, am Institut Städtebau der TU Wien und zuletzt, 2019, an der Sam Fox School des College of Architecture der Washington University in St. Louis, MO, USA. 2009–2016 stand er zudem als Direktor dem Amt für Städtebau der Stadt Zürich vor und verantwortete u. a. die stadträumliche, städtebauliche und architektonische Entwicklung von verschiedenen Stadtgebieten und Arealen in Zürich.

is architect ETH/BSA/SIA and urban planner, co-founder of the architecture firm Steib Gmür Geschwentner Kyburz partners plc. in Zurich, and has chaired the Stuttgart Design Advisory Board in Germany since 2016. He is also regularly invited to be a member of expert juries deciding upon architecture and urban planning competitions in Germany and abroad. In addition, he has held various permanent and visiting professorships; for instance, at the Institute of Architecture, University of Applied Sciences and Arts Northwestern Switzerland FHNW in Muttenz; at the Institute of Urban Design and Landscape Architecture, Faculty for Architecture and Spatial Planning, TU Wien (Austria); and most recently, in 2019, at the College of Architecture, Sam Fox School of Design & Visual Arts, Washington University in St. Louis/MO (USA). From 2009 to 2016 he was Director of the Office for Urban Planning of the City of Zurich and his responsibilities included, for example, the development of urban public space, city planning concepts, and architecture in various city districts and project sites in Zurich.

Christoph Wieser ist Architekt, Publizist, Forscher und Dozent an schweizerischen Fachhochschulen. 2003–2009 war er Redaktor bei *werk, bauen + wohnen*, 2009–2013 Leiter des Instituts Konstruktives Entwerfen der Zürcher Hochschule für Angewandte Wissenschaften ZHAW in Winterthur.

is an architect, author/editor, researcher, and docent at a number of Swiss universities of applied sciences and arts. From 2003 to 2009 he was editor at *werk, bauen + wohnen*, and from 2009 to 2013 he was head of the Institut Konstruktives Entwerfen (Institute of Constructive Design), ZHAW Zürcher Hochschule für Angewandte Wissenschaften (Zurich University of Applied Sciences) in Winterthur.

Tilo Richter ist Architektur- und Kunsthistoriker und seit 1995 als freier Autor und Herausgeber tätig. Daneben ist er Co-Leiter des Verlags Standpunkte, Stiftungsrat von Architektur Dialoge, Redaktor des *Basler Stadtbuchs*, und Mitglied der Redaktionskommission von *werk, bauen + wohnen*.

is a historian of architecture and art and since 1995 has worked as a freelance author/editor. In addition, he is co-director of the publishing association Standpunkte, board member of Architektur Dialoge, editor of the *Basler Stadtbuch*, and member of the editorial commission of *werk, bauen + wohnen*.

Luca Selva ist seit seinem Diplom an der ETH Zürich 1990 selbstständiger Architekt in Basel und war als Assistent an der ETH Zürich (1990–1994), als Professor für Entwurf und Konstruktion an der FHNW (1999–2017) und als Gastprofessor an der MSA Münster (2010–2012) in der Lehre und Forschung tätig. Daneben ist er Mitglied der Stadtbildkommission Basel und weiterer Gremien an der Schnittstelle von Architektur und Kunst, u. a. der Stiftung Schönthal und des Akademierats der Hochschule für Musik in Basel. Zudem ist er in zahlreichen nationalen und internationalen Jurys als Experte für Architektur und Städtebau aktiv. Rege Vortragstätigkeit und Gastkritiken an vielen Hochschulen im In- und Ausland.

has been self-employed as an architect in Basel since graduating from ETH Zurich in 1990. He has also worked as an assistant at the Department of Architecture, ETH Zurich (1990–1994) as professor of design and construction at the Institute of Architecture, University of Applied Sciences and Arts Northwestern Switzerland FHNW in Muttenz (1999–2017); and as visiting professor for teaching and research at MSA Münster School of Architecture, FH Münster—University of Applied Sciences (2010–2012). He is also a member of the Basel Cityscape Commission and other boards at the crossover between architecture and art, including, for instance, the non-profit art and cultural project association Verein Kloster Schönthal and the Akademierat (Academic Board), Academy of Music, University of Applied Sciences and Arts Northwestern Switzerland in Basel. He is also active in numerous national and international juries as an expert in architecture and urban planning, and is frequently invited to give lectures and serve as a guest critic at various national and international universities.

Endnoten
End Notes

1   So wird auch im *Grundrissatlas* und im *Raumpilot*, die sich intensiv mit Wohnungsgrundrissen auseinandersetzen, das Thema nur gestreift. Vgl. Heckmann, Oliver, und Schneider, Friederike (Hg.), *Grundrissatlas Wohnungsbau* (4. überarbeitete und erweiterte Auflage), Basel: 2011; Wüstenrot Stiftung (Hg.), *Raumpilot Wohnen*, Stuttgart, Zürich: 2012.
The topic is only briefly alluded to in *Grundrissatlas Wohnungsbau* and in *Raumpilot Wohnung*, which both deal extensively with residential floor plans. See Oliver Heckmann and Friederike Schneider (eds.), *Grundrissatlas Wohnungsbau*, 4th rev. ed. (Basel: Birkhäuser Verlag, 2011), translated as *Floor Plan Manual Housing*; and Wüstenrot Stiftung (eds.), *Raumpilot Wohnen* (Stuttgart and Zurich: 2012).

2   Vgl.: Trüby, Stephan, *Geschichte des Korridors*, Paderborn: 2018, S. 60.
Stephan Trüby, *Geschichte des Korridors* (Paderborn: 2018), p. 60.

3   Ebenda, S. 44.
Ibid., p. 44.

4   Grabungen im südlichen Jordanien, etwa in Basta, Baja und Beidha, können sogar ins 9. Jahrtausend v. Chr. datiert werden, und in Kharaneh in der jordanischen Wüste liegt ein Fundort mit Hütten, die gar auf 20 000 Jahre geschätzt werden. Vgl. Damals.de, «Vom ersten Grossdorf zum frühislamischen Wüstenschloss», https://www.wissenschaft.de/magazin/weitere-themen/vom-ersten-grossdorf-zum-fruehislamischen-wuestenschloss/ (eingesehen am 17.6.2020); Archäologie online: «20 000 Jahre alte Hütten in Jordanien entdeckt», https://www.archaeologie-online.de/nachrichten/200000-jahre-alte-huetten-in-jordanien-entdeckt-1980/ (eingesehen am 17.6.2020).
Excavated remains in southern Jordan, for instance in Basta, Baja, and Beidha, can even be dated to the 9th millennium BC, and in Khareneh in the Jordanian desert there is a site with huts that are estimated to be twenty thousand years old. See Nadine Riedl, "Vom ersten Grossdorf zum frühislamischen Wüstenschloss," *damals.de*, Sept. 23, 2004, https://www.wissenschaft.de/magazin/weitere-themen/vom-ersten-grossdorf-zum-fruehislamischen-wuestenschloss/ (accessed Sept. 24, 2020); "20 000 Jahre alte Hütten in Jordanien entdeckt," *Archäologie Online*, Feb. 24, 2012, https://www.archaeologie-online.de/nachrichten/200000-jahre-alte-huetten-in-jordanien-entdeckt-1980/ (accessed Sept. 24, 2020).

5   Kose, Arno, «Alter Orient und Ägypten», in: Hoepfner, Wolfram (Hg.), *Geschichte des Wohnens. Band 1: 5000 v. Chr.–500 n. Chr. Vorgeschiche – Frühgeschichte – Antike*, Stuttgart: 1999, S. 18.
Arno Kose, "Alter Orient und Ägypten," in Wolfram Hoepfner (ed.), *Geschichte des Wohnens*, vol. 1: *5000 v. Chr.–500 n. Chr.: Vorgeschichte—Frühgeschichte—Antike* (Stuttgart: 1999), p. 18.

6   Ebenda, S. 24.
Ibid., p. 24.

7   Ebenda, S. 68.
Ibid., p. 68.

8   Hoepfner, Wolfram, und Mitarbeiter, «Die Epoche der Griechen», in: Hoepfner 1999, S. 307.
Wolfram Hoepfner, and assistants, "Die Epoche der Griechen," in Hoepfner, *Geschichte des Wohnens* (see note 5), p. 307.

9   Kose 1999, S. 21.
Kose, "Alter Orient und Ägypten" (see note 5), p. 21.

10 Luley, Helmut, «Wohnen und Wohnungsbau im urgeschichtlichen Mitteleuropa. Die Umgestaltung menschlichen Lebensraums in fünf Jahrtausenden», in: Hoepfner 1999, S. 761.
Helmut Luley, "Wohnen und Wohnungsbau im urgeschichtlichen Mitteleuropa: Die Umgestaltung menschlichen Lebensraums in fünf Jahrtausenden," in Hoepfner, *Geschichte des Wohnens* (see note 5), p. 761.

11 Das Kriterium war u. a. die Anzahl der Feuerstellen: Ab zwei konnten Küche und Stube durch einen Korridor getrennt werden. Vgl. Simonett, Christoph, und Könz, Jachen U., *Die Bauernhäuser des Kantons Graubünden. Band I: Die Wohnbauten* (2. unveränderte Auflage), Basel: 1983, S. 128.
The criteria included the number of hearths or fireplaces: with at least two, the kitchen and living room could be separated by a corridor. See Christoph Simonett, with J. U. Könz, *Die Bauernhäuser des Kantons Graubünden*, vol. I: *Die Wohnbauten*, 2nd ed. (Basel: 1983), p. 128.

12 Von Saldern, Adelheid, «Im Hause, zu Hause. Wohnen im Spannungsfeld von Gegebenheiten und Aneignungen», in: Reulecke, Jürgen (Hg.), *Geschichte des Wohnens. Band 3: 1800–1918. Das bürgerliche Zeitalter*, Stuttgart: 1997, S. 240.
Adelheid von Saldern, "Im Hause, zu Hause: Wohnen im Spannungsfeld von Gegebenheiten und Aneignungen," in Jürgen Reulecke (ed.), *Geschichte des Wohnens*, vol. 3: *1800–1918: Das bürgerliche Zeitalter* (Stuttgart: 1997), p. 240.

13 Seifert, Mathias, «Zur Chronologie und Typologie der Wohnbauten Graubündens im Zeitraum von 1350 bis 1850», in: AS – Archäologie Schweiz et al. (Hg.), *Die Schweiz von 1350 bis 1850 im Spiegel archäologischer Quellen*, Basel: 2018, S. 117.
Mathias Seifert, "Zur Chronologie und Typologie der Wohnbauten Graubündens im Zeitraum von 1350 bis 1850," in AS (Archäologie Schweiz), SAM (Schweizerische Arbeitsgemeinschaft für die Archäologie des Mittelalters und der Neuzeit), and SBV (Schweizerischer Burgenverein) (eds.), *Die Schweiz von 1350 bis 1850 im Spiegel archäologischer Quellen* (Basel: 2018), p. 117.

14 Ebenda, S. 117.
Ibid., p. 117.

15 Roth reklamiert diese Typologie für sich. Sie basiert aber auf dem sogenannten Schustertyp, den Franz Schuster in Niederursel 1928 erstmals angewandt hatte. Vgl. Risse, Heike, *Frühe Moderne in Frankfurt am Main 1920–1933*, Frankfurt a. M.: 1984, S. 44.
Roth claims to have invented this typology himself. However, it is based on the so-called "Schuster type," which Viennese architect Franz Schuster first used in the school in Niederursel, Frankfurt am Main, in 1928. See Heike Risse, *Frühe Moderne in Frankfurt am Main 1920–1933* (Frankfurt a. M.: 1984), p. 44.

16 Roth, Alfred, *Das Neue Schulhaus* (3. Auflage), Stuttgart: 1961, S. 39.
Alfred Roth, *Das Neue Schulhaus/The New School/La nouvelle école*, 3rd ed., English transl. William B. Gleckman (Zurich: 1961), p. 38.

17 Beckel, Inge, «Im Zentrum steht der Mensch. Gedanken zum Strukturalismus der Nachkriegsarchitektur», in: TEC21, Heft 8, 2002, S. 7 und 10.
Inge Beckel, "Im Zentrum steht der Mensch: Gedanken zum Strukturalismus der Nachkriegsarchitektur," in TEC21, 8 (2002), p. 7 and 10.

18 Hufnagl, Viktor, *Bauten – Projekte – Gedanken – Theorie – Erfahrungen – Erkenntnisse 1950–2000*, Wien: 2001, S. 93.
Viktor Hufnagl, *Buildings – Projects, Experience – Insights, Ideas – Theory: 1950–2000*, English transl. Maria E. Clay-Jorde (Vienna: 2001), p. 93.

19 Mack, Gerhard, *Herzog & de Meuron 1978–1988 (Das Gesamtwerk. Band 1)*, Basel, Boston, Berlin: 1997, S. 57.
Gerhard Mack (ed.), *Herzog & de Meuron: Das Gesamtwerk/The Complete Works*, vol. 1: *1978–1988* (Basel, Boston and Berlin: 1997), p. 57.

20 Le Corbusier und Jeanneret, Pierre, *Œuvre complète 1910–1929*, Zürich: 1960, S. 128.
W. Boesiger and O. Stonorov (eds.), *Le Corbusier and Pierre Jeanneret: Œuvre complète 1910–1929*, 7th ed. (Zurich: 1960), p. 128.

21 Beckel, Inge, «Urbanisierung einer Hafenanlage. Wohnbauten von Diener & Diener Architekten in Amsterdam», in: *Schweizer Ingenieur und Architekt*, Heft 11, 1997, S. 9.
Inge Beckel, "Urbanisierung einer Hafenanlage: Wohnbauten von Diener & Diener Architekten in Amsterdam," in SI+A/*Schweizer Ingenieur und Architekt*, 115, no. 11 (March 13, 1997), p. 205.

22 Heckmann, Oliver, ««The Sweetness of Functioning is Architecture»: über den Gebrauch von Grundrissen», in: Heckmann und Schneider 2011, S. 9.
Oliver Heckmann, "'The Sweetness of Functioning is Architecture': On the Use of Floor Plans," in Oliver Heckmann and Friederike Schneider (eds.), *Floor Plan Manual Housing*, 4th rev. ed. (Basel: 2011), p. 9.

23 Die Unterteilung verweist darauf, dass der Palast im Innern in zwei gleich grosse Hälften geteilt ist, die je über eine separate Treppe erschlossen werden. Vgl. Markschies, Alexander, *Gebaute Pracht. Der Palazzo Strozzi in Florenz (1489–1534)*, Freiburg im Breisgau: 2000, S. 47.
The subdivision indicates that the interior of the palace is divided into two halves of equal size, each accessible by a separate staircase. See Alexander Markschies, *Gebaute Pracht: Der Palazzo Strozzi in Florenz (1489–1534)* (Freiburg im Breisgau: 2000), p. 47.

24 Trüby 2018, S. 69.
Trüby, *Geschichte des Korridors* (see note 2), p. 69.

25 Faber, Tobias, *Dansk Arkitektur*, Kopenhagen: 1963, S. 168.
Tobias Faber, *Dansk Arkitektur* (Copenhagen: 1963), p. 168.

26 Das ist ja auch der typologische Unterschied zur Galerie, die ursprünglich ein längsrechteckiger, korridorartiger Raum war. Vgl. Von Naredi-Rainer, Paul, «Museumstypologie – Ein architekturgeschichtlicher Abriss», in: *Detail*, Heft 9, 2006, S. 932.
This is also how it differs typologically from the traditional gallery, which was originally a rectangular, corridor-like room. See Paul von Naredi-Rainer, "Museumstypologie: Ein architekturgeschichtlicher Abriss," *Detail*, 46, no. 9 (2006), p. 932.

27 Leuenberger, Gottlieb, et al. (Hg.), *Sozialer Wohnungs- und Siedlungsbau* (Schriftenreihe zur Frage der Arbeitsbeschaffung. Bautechnische Reihe, Nr. 9), Zürich: 1944, S. 24.
G. Leuenberger, et al. (eds.), *Sozialer Wohnungs- und Siedlungsbau*, no. 9 in the Bautechnische Reihe: Schriftenreihe zur Frage der Arbeitsbeschaffung (Zurich: 1944), p. 24.

28 Claus, Sylvia, et al. (Hg.), *Lux Guyer 1894–1955 Architektin*, Zürich: 2013, S. 234.
Sylvia Claus, Dorothee Huber, and Beate Schnitter (eds.), *Lux Guyer 1894–1955: Architektin* (Zurich: 2009), p. 234.

29 Gangler, Anette, *Ein traditionelles Wohnviertel im Nordosten der Altstadt von Aleppo in Nordsyrien*, Tübingen, Berlin: 1993, S. 77.
Anette Gangler, *Ein traditionelles Wohnviertel im Nordosten der Altstadt von Aleppo in Nordsyrien* (Tübingen and Berlin: 1993), p. 77.

30 Ebenda, S. 94.
Ibid., p. 94.

31 Ebenda, S. 74.
Ibid., p. 74.

32 Ebenda, S. 53.
Ibid., p. 53.

33 So auch bei einem der ältesten Gebäude im Quartier (1788), das in zwei separate Häuser getrennt und laufend verändert wurde. Siehe ebenda, S. 95.
This is also the case with one of the oldest buildings in the quarter (1788), which was divided into two separate houses and repeatedly changed. See Ibid., p. 95.

34 Ingenieurschule beider Basel Abteilung Architektur (Hg.), *Soglio. Siedlungen und Bauten* (zweite, erweiterte Auflage). Basel, Boston, Berlin: 1997. Treibende Kraft hinter dem Projekt waren Michael Alder und Diego Giovanoli, Mitarbeiter der Denkmalpflege Graubünden.
Ingenieurschule beider Basel, Abteilung Architektur (ed.), *Soglio: Siedlungen und Bauten*, 2nd expanded ed. (Basel, Boston and Berlin: 1997). The driving forces behind the project were Michael Alder, Basel architect and docent for architecture at the IBB, and Diego Giovanoli, employee at the Canton of Graubünden Department of Historic Preservation.

35 Ebenda, S. 43.
Ibid., p. 43.

36 Ebenda, S. 23.
Ibid., p. 23.

37 Spiro, Annette, und Ganzoni, David (Hg.), *Der Bauplan*, Zürich: 2013, S. 6–7.
Annette Spiro, "The Working Drawing," in Annette Spiro and David Ganzoni (eds.), *The Working Drawing: The Architect's Tool* (Zurich: 2013), p. 6–7.

Bildnachweis
Image Credits

1	aus/from Frampton, Kenneth, *Grundlagen der Architektur. Studien zur Kultur des Tektonischen*, München/Stuttgart: 1993.
2	aus/from Hoepfner, Wolfram (Hg.), *Geschichte des Wohnens. Band 1: 5000 v. Chr.–500 n. Chr. Vorgeschichte – Frühgeschichte – Antike*, Stuttgart: 1999.
3	aus/from Hoepfner, Wolfram (Hg.), *Geschichte des Wohnens. Band 1: 5000 v. Chr.–500 n. Chr. Vorgeschichte – Frühgeschichte – Antike*, Stuttgart: 1999.
4	Luca Selva Architekten
5	Luca Selva Architekten Fotografie/photography: © Adriano Biondo
6	Luca Selva Architekten
7	aus/from Hoepfner, Wolfram (Hg.), *Geschichte des Wohnens. Band 1: 5000 v. Chr.–500 n. Chr. Vorgeschichte – Frühgeschichte – Antike*, Stuttgart: 1999.
8	Luca Selva Architekten
9	Luca Selva Architekten
10	aus/from Hoepfner, Wolfram (Hg.), *Geschichte des Wohnens. Band 1: 5000 v. Chr.–500 n. Chr. Vorgeschichte – Frühgeschichte – Antike*, Stuttgart: 1999.
11	aus/from Hoepfner, Wolfram (Hg.), *Geschichte des Wohnens. Band 1: 5000 v. Chr.–500 n. Chr. Vorgeschichte – Frühgeschichte – Antike*, Stuttgart: 1999.
12	Luca Selva Architekten
13	Luca Selva Architekten Fotografie/photography: © Ruedi Walti
14	aus/from Hoepfner, Wolfram (Hg.), *Geschichte des Wohnens. Band 1: 5000 v. Chr.–500 n. Chr. Vorgeschichte – Frühgeschichte – Antike*, Stuttgart: 1999.
18	aus/from Hoepfner, Wolfram (Hg.), *Geschichte des Wohnens. Band 1: 5000 v. Chr.–500 n. Chr. Vorgeschichte – Frühgeschichte – Antike*, Stuttgart: 1999.
19/20	Luca Selva Architekten
21	aus/from Simonett, Christoph, Könz, Jachen U., *Die Bauernhäuser des Kantons Graubünden. Band I: Die Wohnbauten* (2. unveränderte Auflage), Basel: 1983.
22	Luca Selva Architekten Fotografie/photography: © Roman Weyeneth
23	Luca Selva Architekten
24	aus/from Reulecke, Jürgen (Hg.), *Geschichte des Wohnens. Band 3: 1800–1918. Das bürgerliche Zeitalter*, Stuttgart: 1997.
25	aus/from Ruch, Hans-Jörg, *Historische Häuser im Engadin. Architektonische Interventionen von Hans-Jörg Ruch*, Zürich: 2009.
26	Luca Selva Architekten
27	aus/from Roth, Alfred, *Das Neue Schulhaus* (3. Auflage), Stuttgart: 1961.
28	aus/from Hufnagel, Viktor, *Bauten – Projekte – Gedanken – Theorie – Erfahrungen – Erkenntnisse 1950–2000*, Wien: 2001.
32	Herzog & de Meuron
36	Fondation Le Corbusier, Paris
39	Fondation Le Corbusier, Paris
45	Diener & Diener Architekten, Basel
46	Luca Selva Architekten Fotografie/photography: © Yohan Zerdoun
50	aus/from Heckmann, Oliver, Schneider, Friederike (Hg.), *Grundrissatlas Wohnungsbau* (4. überarbeitete und erweiterte Auflage), Basel: 2011.
53	aus/from Muthesius, Hermann, *Das Englische Haus. Entwicklungen, Bedingungen, Anlage, Aufbau Einrichtung und Innenraum in 3 Bänden* (Band I), Berlin: 1904.
56	Luca Selva Architekten Fotografie/photography: © Yohan Zerdoun
57	Luca Selva Architekten
58	Luca Selva Architekten
59	Luca Selva Architekten
60	Luca Selva Architekten
61	Luca Selva Architekten
62	aus/from Studer, Heinz, *Baustilkunde. Entwicklung der Baustile vom alten ägyptischen Reich bis Ende 20. Jahrhundert, Schweizer Baudokumentation* (3. Auflage), Blauen: 1987.
63	Luca Selva Architekten
64	aus/from Frommel, Christoph Luitpold, *Der Palazzo Venezia in Rom*, Opladen: 1982.
65	aus/from Faber, Tobias, *Dansk Arkitektur*, Kopenhagen: 1963.
66	Luca Selva Architekten Fotografie/photography: © Yohan Zerdoun
73	Architekturmuseum der TU München
74	aus/from Von Moos, Stanislaus, *Venturi Scott Brown & Associates. Buildings and Projects 1986–1998*, New York: 1999.
80	aus/from Leuenberger, G., et al., *Sozialer Wohnungs- und Siedlungsbau* (Schriftenreihe zur Frage der Arbeitsbeschaffung. Bautechnische Reihe, Nr. 9), Zürich: 1944.
85	Luca Selva Architekten Fotografie/photography: © Ruedi Walti
88	aus/from Risselada, Max, *Raumplan versus Plan Libre*, Delft: 1987.
94	ETH Zürich, Institut gta, gta-Archiv
95/96	Luca Selva Architekten
97	Luca Selva Architekten
98/99	aus/from Gangler, Anette, *Ein traditionelles Wohnviertel im Nordosten der Altstadt von Aleppo in Nordsyrien*, Tübingen, Berlin: 1993.
100	aus/from Gangler, Anette, *Ein traditionelles Wohnviertel im Nordosten der Altstadt von Aleppo in Nordsyrien*, Tübingen, Berlin: 1993.
101	Luca Selva Architekten
102/103	aus/from Ingenieurschule beider Basel, Abteilung Architektur (Hg.), *Soglio. Siedlungen und Bauten* (2. erweiterte Auflage), Basel, Boston, Berlin: 1997.
104	Luca Selva Architekten Fotografie/photography: © Ruedi Walti
105/106	Luca Selva Architekten

Impressum
Inprint

Herausgeber
Editors
Tilo Richter,
Christoph Wieser

Texte und Bildlegenden
Texts and captions
Luca Selva,
Christoph Wieser

Gespräch
Interview
Patrick Gmür,
Luca Selva

Bildlegenden Luca Selva Architekten
Captions Luca Selva Architekten
Tilo Richter,
Luca Selva

Konzept
Concept
Anic Aklin,
Tilo Richter,
Luca Selva,
Christoph Wieser

Konzept und Gestaltung
Concept and graphic design
Bonbon, Zürich
Valeria Bonin,
Diego Bontognali,
Basil Knill

Übersetzung
Translations
Linda Cassens Stoian, Basel

Lektorat
Copy editing
Maike Kleihauer/
Thomas Skelton-Robinson

Korrektorat
Proofreading
Miriam Seifert-Waibel
Dean Drake

Lithografie, Druck und Bindung
Pre-press, printing and binding
DZA Druckerei zu Altenburg GmbH,
Altenburg, Thüringen

© 2021 Park Books AG, Zürich

© für die Texte: die Autorinnen und Autoren
© for the texts: the authors

Park Books
Niederdorfstrasse 54
8001 Zürich
Schweiz / Switzerland
www.park-books.com

Park Books wird vom Bundesamt für Kultur mit einem Strukturbeitrag für die Jahre 2021–2024 unterstützt.
Park Books is being supported by the Federal Office of Culture with a general subsidy for the years 2021–2024.

Alle Rechte vorbehalten; kein Teil dieses Werks darf in irgendeiner Form ohne vorherige schriftliche Genehmigung des Verlags reproduziert oder unter Verwendung elektronischer Systeme verarbeitet, vervielfältigt oder verbreitet werden.
All rights reserved; no part of this publication may be reproduced, stored in a retrieval system or transmitted in any form or by any means, electronic, mechanical, photocopying, recording, or otherwise, without the prior written consent of the publisher.

ISBN 978-3-03860-208-8